D0758808

SACRAMENTO PUBLIC LIBRARY
3 3029 00527 5052
CEN R843 S589zy 1976
1
Young, Trud Georges Simenon : a
Scarecrow Press, 1976.
3 3029 00527 5052

The Scarecrow Author Bibliographies

1. John Steinbeck (Tetsumaro Hayashi). 1973.
2. Joseph Conrad (Theodore G. Ehrsam). 1969.
3. Arthur Miller (Tetsumaro Hayashi). 2d ed. due 1976.
4. Katherine Anne Porter (Waldrip & Bauer). 1969.
5. Philip Freneau (Philip M. Marsh). 1970.
6. Robert Greene (Tetsumaro Hayashi). 1971.
7. Benjamin Disraeli (R. W. Stewart). 1972.
8. John Berryman (Richard W. Kelly). 1972.
9. William Dean Howells (Vito J. Brenni). 1973.
10. Jean Anouilh (Kathleen W. Kelly). 1973.
11. E. M. Forster (Alfred Borrello). 1973.
12. The Marquis de Sade (E. Pierre Chanover). 1973.
13. Alain Robbe-Grillet (Dale W. Fraizer). 1973.
14. Northrop Frye (Robert D. Denham). 1974.
15. Federico García Lorca (Laurenti & Siracusa). 1974.
16. Ben Jonson (Brock & Welsh). 1974.
17. Four French Dramatists: Eugène Brieux, François de Curel, Emile Fabre, Paul Hervieu (Edmund F. SantaVicca). 1974.
18. Ralph Waldo Ellison (Jacqueline Covo). 1974.
19. Philip Roth (Bernard F. Rodgers, Jr.). 1974.
20. Norman Mailer (Laura Adams). 1974.
21. Sir John Betjeman (Margaret Stapleton). 1974.
22. Elie Wiesel (Molly Abramowitz). 1974.
23. Paul Laurence Dunbar (Eugene W. Metcalf, Jr.). 1975.
24. Henry James (Beatrice Ricks). 1975.
25. Robert Frost (Lentricchia & Lentricchia). 1976.
26. Sherwood Anderson (Douglas G. Rogers). 1976.
27. Iris Murdoch and Muriel Spark (Tominaga and Schneidermeyer). 1976.
28. John Ruskin (Kirk H. Beetz). 1976.
29. Georges Simenon (Trudee Young). 1976.

GEORGES SIMENON:

A checklist of his "Maigret" and other mystery novels and short stories in French and in English translations

by

TRUDEE YOUNG

The Scarecrow Author Bibliographies, No. 29

The Scarecrow Press, Inc.
Metuchen, N.J. 1976

Library of Congress Cataloging in Publication Data

Young, Trudee.
Georges Simenon : a checklist of his "Maigret" and other mystery novels and short stories in French and in English translations.

(The Scarecrow author bibliographies ; no. 29)
Includes indexes.
1. Simenon, Georges, 1903- --Bibliography.
Z8819.147.Y68 [PQ2637.I53] 016.8439'1'2
ISBN 0-8108-0964-8 76-14410

Printed in the United States of America

CONTENTS

Part I: Biography 1

Part II: Introduction to the Checklist 7

Part III: Checklist 13
- Titles First Published in the 1930s 13
- Titles First Published in the 1940s 51
- Titles First Published in the 1950s 77
- Titles First Published in the 1960s 113
- Titles First Published in the 1970s 133

Appendix: Sources for Part III 138

Indexes 141
- French Titles 141
- English Translations 148

PART I

BIOGRAPHY

Georges Simenon may well be the most prolific writer of the twentieth century. This Belgian-born author, best known as a writer of detective novels and the creator of the character Chief Inspector Maigret, has written over 200 novels and short stories (detective as well as "serious" novels), plus an additional 208 books written early in his career under pseudonyms. Although Simenon has written a vast number of stories, he is not as well-known an author in this country today as he was during the 1950s when he lived and wrote in the United States. Before discussing the reasons for compiling a checklist of Simenon's works and the methodology and sources used, it seems appropriate, therefore, to provide a description of the man and his writing career, as well as a general overview of his work.

Georges Joseph Christian Simenon was born in Liège, Belgium, February 13, 1903, of a French father and a Dutch mother. As early as age thirteen, he expressed the desire to devote his life to writing. He did not feel that writing was a career, so he decided to become either a priest or a soldier, because it seemed to Simenon that they had time to themselves during the day. At sixteen he was forced to quit school when his father died suddenly. His mother then apprenticed him to a pastry cook, but he stayed there for only a year and then took a job as a reporter for the Liège Gazette. It was not long after becoming a newspaper reporter that he wrote his first novel, Au Pont des Arches, which was a satire on Liège society.

In 1922 he left Liège and moved to Paris where he decided to devote all of his time to writing. He went daily to submit his stories to Colette, who was at that time editor of the newspaper Le Matin, but she refused them. She gave him some advice, though, that actually proved to be very important to Simenon's writing career. She told him that his writing was too literary. The public did not read heavy literature, but preferred to read a good story, and that is what a writer should be able to do: tell a good story in a simple and clear way.

According to Simenon, it took him about ten years of writing (from 1923 to 1933) to learn how to tell a good story; those years he referred to as his apprenticeship. Simenon turned his writing away from the very "literary" to the popular novel or "pulp" fiction, as it is called. He wrote at least 80 pages of copy a day. It has been estimated that he produced 208 popular novels, most of which were published in pulp magazines, and he also used at least seventeen different pen names: Aramis, Christian Brulls, Germain d'Antibes, Luc Dorsan, Jacques Dersonnes, Jacques Dossage, Jean Dorsange, Georges Caraman, Georges d'Isly, Gom Gut, Kim, Georges Martin Georges, Jean du Perry, Maurice Pertius, Poum and Zetta, Plick and Plock, Jean Sandor, Georges Sim and Gaston Vialis.

All of the writing he did during the 1920s not only gave him a chance to perfect his style, but it also made him rich enough to be able to live well in Paris and have a chauffeur-driven car. Simenon wanted to be able to have these things because they would allow him to broaden his learning experiences. His philosophy of writing then, as explained later during a speech delivered at the French Institute of New York in 1945 (the text of which is available in the _French Review_ 19 [February 1946]: pp. 212-229), was that a writer was _only_ able to transmit to his readers those experiences he had himself lived.

Simenon, therefore, needed the means to be able to learn about all facets of the world, both horizontally and vertically. That is to say, he wanted to be able to travel throughout the world and come in contact with its different countries, peoples, climates, ways of life, as well as to have access to different levels of society--to feel at ease in the local bar as well as in a banker's living room. Thus, in the late 1920s, with the money he had earned from writing "pulp" fiction, he bought himself a yacht, which he named the OSTROGOT, and traveled all around Europe. It was during these travels that he wrote his first detective novel, _Pietr-Le-Letton_ (_The Strange Case of Peter the Lett_), in which he created the character of Inspector Maigret.

Simenon wrote three other Maigret novels during the time he was sailing around Europe. In 1931 he decided to have his detective novels published. He took them to Fayard, a Parisian publishing company which had published some of his earlier popular novels. He told the editor that these stories represented a new type of fiction which he called the "semi-literary" novel. He was finished with writing "pulp" fiction, and he was ready to move onto another genre. Although Fayard agreed to publish his Maigret novels, and Simenon signed a contract to produce one detective novel per month, the editors were still not sure whether the public would like these detective novels. They were not like other detective novels. The main character, Inspector Maigret--a heavy-set, pipe-smoking detective--did not use scientific means to solve his cases, only his intuition; there were no love affairs; there were no truly good guys and bad guys; and, finally, the story ended neither bad nor good.

These doubts proved unfounded, however, and Simenon's Maigret novels became popular in Europe. Unfortunately, only a few of his Maigrets during the thirties were translated into English and made available in the United States. It was not until the 1940s, when Harcourt decided to publish Simenon's works, that his Maigret novels became known to Americans.

After writing about twenty Maigrets, Simenon broke his contract with Fayard. He was tired of the character of Maigret and just wanted to write novels. It was time for Simenon to move on again to another literary genre. Actually, the transition from writing detective novels to "straight" novels ("romans tout court") was not as abrupt as it seems. As he continued his Maigret series, he increasingly applied his skill in the economical use of words, the brief but vivid descriptions and the cohesion between characters and background. His stories became more like psychological studies, focusing on the characters rather than the action.

In 1933 he abandoned Inspector Maigret and wrote a book called Les Gens d'en Face, the first in a series of novels ("romans d'atmosphère") written during the 1930s in which the action revolves around the Russian seaport of Batum, and the depiction of customs and characters assumes an importance that it had not had in his earlier works. After writing this book, Simenon felt that he was finally beginning his literary career. As other books appeared--Le Coup de Lune in 1933 and Les Pitard in 1935--Simenon was gradually emerging as the writer of singularly gripping psychological studies. These works were what he called the "romans-crise"--novels which concentrate on one or two principal characters depicted in moments of sharp crisis.

After spending World War II in France, he traveled to the United States where he lived and wrote until 1955. All during the 1940s and 1950s Simenon's writing went back and forth between the serious, psychological novel and the Maigret novel. This pattern continued throughout his writing career; he never seemed to be able to let go of the character of Chief Inspector Maigret. He even brought Maigret to this country, involving him in situations all over the United States. Simenon was at the height of his popularity here while he was living and writing on his farm in Connecticut. Then in 1955 he went back to Europe, choosing to live this time in Switzerland, where he is presently living. After that the name of Georges Simenon became less widely known to Americans.

Although he became less familiar to Americans after his return to Europe, Simenon did not slow down his writing career during the 1960s. He continued writing both Maigret and non-Maigret stories at his usual pace--three or four novels per year. By this time, though, the critics had decided that Simenon was never going to be the literary figure they had anticipated, and they paid little attention to his writing, other than keeping track of the quantity. By the early 1970s, certain literary critics were becoming rather critical of Simenon's writing, stating that he made too many errors and was also too out of touch with the modern world. It was no longer the 1930s, and Inspector Maigret was no longer a believable character. Finally, Simenon decided that it was time to stop writing; it was too much of a strain, and he announced his retirement in February, 1973, at the age of 70. He even went to the Belgian consulate to change the designation of his profession on his passport from novelist to "sans profession."

Simenon devoted more than 50 years of his life to writing, and he produced an enormous amount of fiction--over 400 novels and short stories. How does one explain such a prolific output? It has been explained best, perhaps by Simenon himself, during an interview with Harvey Breit which appeared in the New York Times Book Review, May 28, 1950. He said that a writer is an artist who must learn his craft and does so by writing a lot. He also said that he had a definite need to write, which hits him as a kind of "disequilibrium." There was something about this man, though, that made him special. Maybe it was the fact that when he was not writing, he was absorbing life as a sponge absorbs water. When he would begin to write, he would squeeze the sponge and out it came, not water but ink.

There is one other aspect of the man that needs to be discussed, and that is his method of writing novels. Every writer has his own ritual that he follows, especially a writer like Simenon who wrote so much material.

The day before Simenon was to write a novel, he would take a walk, as he did every day. But he would not really see the scenery around him, as he did on other days. It was as if he were in a trance. He would meet the same people he was used to seeing and greeting on other days during his walks, but he would forget to greet them. After he finished walking and arrived home, he would go to his soundproof office and write down a few names on a piece of paper, so as not to forget them when he began writing the following morning. He would note their ages, telephone numbers and addresses, because these were real characters, and he felt it was necessary to give them their total identity. Then, perhaps, he would put up a small map of the town or region where the action was to take place, and often he would have a train schedule close at hand, since in real life someone always is going somewhere. Finally, he would prepare his writing materials to be ready for the following day's work.

The next day he would wake up early and begin writing, without even eating. Two hours later he would complete his first chapter, usually twenty pages in length, and within eleven days he would complete the entire novel and send a copy to his publisher. If there were ever any interruption that kept him away from his work for as much as 48 hours, the spell was broken and he would throw away everything that he had written.

During the eleven-day period when he was writing a novel, he would be totally immersed in the story. Simenon created the people for his story, placed them in their milieu and left them to live. According to Simenon, he had no control over his characters and the type of story they were going to tell during the course of the eleven days.

When he decided finally to stop writing, it was a sad day for many avid Simenon readers. He certainly had many admirers during his writing career, one of them being André

Gide, who regularly read Simenon's works. Gide, in fact, decided to devote some of his time to doing a critical study of Simenon. Every time Gide read one of Simenon's novels, he would take notes and then send his reactions to Simenon. They exchanged letters for about ten years.

This biographical sketch and general overview of Simenon's work ends, then, with an excerpt from Andre Gide's diary which expresses what one person, a fellow author, liked about Simenon's writing, and what, perhaps, other readers have also found to be true:

13 January, 1948

> ... Simenon's subjects often have a profound psychological and ethical interest, but insufficiently indicated, as if he were not aware of their importance himself, or as if he expected the reader to catch the hint. This is what attracts and holds me in him. He writes for 'the vast public,' to be sure, but delicate and refined readers find something for them too as soon as they begin to take him seriously. He makes one reflect; and this is close to being the height of art; how superior he is in this to those heavy novelists who do not spare us a single commentary! Simenon sets forth a particular fact, perhaps of general interest; but he is careful not to generalize; that is up to the reader.[1]

1Gide, André. The Journals of André Gide. Volume 4: 1939-1949. Translated by Justin O'Brien (New York: Knopf, 1951), p. 287.

PART II

INTRODUCTION TO CHECKLIST

The purpose of this checklist is to provide libraries with a listing of the major French editions and English translations of Simenon's detective and "serious" novels as an aid in selection and acquisition. Collectors of Simenon's writings, of course, will also find this checklist to be helpful as a starting place for locating the major editions of his works. This checklist attempts to provide a single listing of those editions appearing in the major French, English and American national and trade bibliographies, as well as complete bibliographic data for each item. The listing is not complete nor, probably, without error, since the compiler was not able to examine every edition.

Because of the quantity of material Simenon has produced and the time factor involved in compiling this checklist, some restrictions were placed on its scope. Only those novels, short stories and nonfiction works written under his real name are included in this checklist. None of his pseudonymous works is included, because they are not readily available in this country. A large portion of the pseudonymous works were published in French "pulp" magazines and are not now obtainable. Also, the checklist does not include other adaptations, such as movies, that have been made from his novels, although there are two of his works for which dramatic adaptations were found, but these were published in periodicals. For these other adaptations the reader is referred to the book, Simenon, written by Bernard de Fallois (Paris: Gallimard, 1961), which includes a rather extensive bibliography of Simenon's fiction written before 1960, movie adaptations, nonfiction, and critical studies on his work. For a more recent list of movie and theatrical adaptations, there is the bibliography done by C. Menguy which appeared in Adam International Review (vol. 34, nos. 328-330, 1969) entitled "Bibliographie filmographie et adaptations théâtrales de Georges Simenon."

Previous Bibliographic Research

The most complete bibliographies of Simenon's first editions and pseudonymous works are those compiled by A. Grisay and C. Menguy and published in the Belgian serial Livre et l'Estampe (Société des Bibliophiles et Iconophiles de Belgique):

Grisay, A. "Bibliographie des éditions originales de Georges Simenon," Livre et l'Estampe, No. 37, 1964, pp. 5-34.

Grisay, A. and C. Menguy. "Bibliographie des éditions originales de Georges Simenon y compris des oeuvres publiées sous pseudonymes," Livre et l'Estampe, Nos. 49/50, 1967, pp. 5-84.

Menguy, C. "Additions et corrections à la bibliographie des éditions originales de Georges Simenon," Livre et l'Estampe, Nos. 67/68, 1971, pp. 186-206.

Other bibliographic research on Simenon has been done by various European literary critics who have included a listing of Simenon's novels as part of their critical studies of Simenon's style. These bibliographies are helpful as a starting place for determining titles, as they are more available for use here, but they do not provide complete bibliographic data on each title. These include:

de Fallois, Bernard. Simenon. Paris: Gallimard, 1961.

Narcejac, Thomas. The Art of Simenon. Translated by Cynthia Rowland. London: Routledge and Kegan Paul, 1952.

Raymond, John. Simenon in Court. London: Hamish Hamilton, 1968.

Ritzen, Quentin. Simenon, Avocat des Hommes. Paris: Le Livre Contemporain, 1961.

Stéphanie, Roger. Le Dossier Simenon. Paris: Laffont, 1961.

Thoorens, Leon. Qui Etes-Vous Georges Simenon? Verviers: Gerard, 1959.

The Fallois bibliography, as mentioned earlier in this chapter, is very helpful in locating pseudonymous works, critical studies, nonfiction, Maigret and non-detective novels written under his real name before 1960. The Narcejac bibliography is not as complete as the one by Fallois, but it is useful in locating English translations, as his list includes both the French first editions and the English translations (including the imprint and date of publication for both). Of course, Narcejac's bibliography is not up-to-date. One can go then to John Raymond's bibliography to locate both the French titles and English translations published up to 1967.

There are also two American sources which include bibliographies of Simenon's English translations published in Great Britain and the United States. The first was compiled by Ordean A. Hagen and appears in his book Who Done It? A Guide to Detective, Mystery and Suspense Fiction (New York: Bowker, 1969). Hagen's bibliography on Simenon is rather complete and includes English translations published up to 1968. Unfortunately there is no reference to the original French title.

The second source, although not very complete, is the book entitled A Catalogue of Crime, by Jacques Barzun and Wendell Hertig Taylor (New York: Harper & Row, 1971). This is an annotated list of all types of mystery novels. Coverage of Simenon includes selections from both his Maigret and non-Maigret novels. The Hagen bibliography is more helpful in locating English translations then the Barzun and Taylor list. Both of these works are important studies, from both a bibliographic and a critical point of view, of this not always appreciated literary genre.

Methodology and Important Sources

The methodology for compiling this checklist was divided into two sections: 1) determining and listing French titles and their editions; 2) determining and listing English translations. First of all, a list of French titles appearing in the Fallois, Narcejac and Raymond bibliographies was compiled in order to provide some sort of a beginning reference point. Then the French national and trade bibliographies were consulted to verify the publication date of the first editions and to obtain complete bibliographic data for each edition.

After the French titles had been adequately searched,

a list of English translations and their original French titles was obtained from the Narcejac and Raymond bibliographies. As with the first list of French titles, this list of English translations served as a beginning reference point. Then the British national and trade bibliographies were searched, followed by the American ones. In order to search these national bibliographies successfully, it was necessary to make a complete list of French titles along with the translated English titles, since only a few of the sources provided the original French title along with the translation.

The most useful sources for locating first editions of Simenon's works in French up to 1947 was the Catalogue Général des Livres Imprimés de la Bibliothèque Nationale. The bibliographic data found here for each title included the imprint, date of publication and the collection. Another very useful source for locating French editions was the trade bibliography, Biblio, Catalogue des Ouvrages Parus en Langue Française dans le Monde Entier. Biblio included not only those editions of Simenon published in France, but also those published in the French language in other countries throughout the world. Its coverage is from 1934 to the present.

For the English translations, the British Museum book catalogs turned out to be a good starting point since they include the original French title for many of the translations up to 1970. The Cumulative Book Index was very helpful in locating American editions as well as the British editions of the translations. Being a trade bibliography, the CBI's entries were more complete than those in the British Museum book catalogs. The American Book Publishing Record was a helpful source for determining the original French titles for the English translations, especially the American editions, of works published after 1960, since it also listed the original French titles. The British National Bibliography gave good coverage of the British editions of the English translations published after 1950, with complete bibliographic data included. Finally, the Library of Congress book catalogs were a good source for obtaining information on unusual editions in the original French.

Organization

The checklist is arranged chronologically by the year the French title was first published. All titles published during the same year are further arranged alphabetically.

Both the French editions and the English translations are listed together under each title, the French editions appearing first in chronological order followed by the English translations (British editions followed by the American editions). For the collected works, such as short stories, only those short stories that were also published separately are listed as separate entries in the bibliography. Otherwise they are listed with the collection title. There is also an index to both the French and English titles.

Two final points need to be explained. One is the problem of the collation and the other is the use of the terms "deluxe" editions or editions printed on special paper. First, there was much variation in the collations given in the various national and trade bibliographies, especially for French editions published during the same year. It was difficult to determine whether the differences in the collation were due to different methods of counting pages or to the existence of other editions, since not all of the editions were available for inspection. Generally, throughout the listing, though, the pagination listed in Biblio is given for editions published the same year, in cases where there was any doubt. Because Simenon wrote so many novels, it is difficult to know how many of the editions for the different titles actually made their way into various national and trade bibliographies of France, Great Britain and the United States.

As for the use of the terms "deluxe" editions ("éditions de luxe") or editions printed on special paper, these are actually limited editions published on special paper in order to make more money on a few purchases. As explained by Adrian Goldstone, who has a large private collection of mystery novels, "priority of issue is usually claimed for the limited copies, but, as they are always printed out of the same setting of type, they are seldom given great preference by modern bibliographers unless signed by the author and are variants of the editions."[1]

[1]Letter from Adrian H. Goldstone to Dr. Stuart Baillie, April 18, 1975.

SOURCES FOR PARTS I AND II

Bibliographical Index; A Cumulative Bibliography of Bibliographies, 1938- . New York: H. W. Wilson, 1938- .

Breit, Harvey. "Talk with Simenon," New York Times Book Review, May 28, 1950, p. 17.

Fellows, Otis, ed. Tournants Dangereux. New York: Appleton Century Crofts, 1953.

Gide, Andre. The Journals of André Gide. Volume 4: 1939-1949. Translated by Justin O'Brien. New York: Knopf, 1951.

Letter from Adrian H. Goldstone to Dr. Stuart Baillie, April 18, 1975.

Loriot, Noelle. "L'Adieu de Georges Simenon," L'Express, February 19, 1973, p. 73.

Loriot, Noelle. "Qu'est arrivé à Georges Simenon?" L'Express, October 16, 1972, p. 74.

Moritz, Charles, ed. Current Biography Yearbook, 1970. New York: H. W. Wilson, 1971.

"Newsmakers," Newsweek, February 19, 1973, pp. 54-55.

Raymond, John. Simenon in Court. London: Hamish Hamilton, 1968.

Simenon, Georges. "Le Romancier," French Review 19 (February 1946): pp. 212-229.

PART III

CHECKLIST

Titles First Published in the 1930s

1931

1. AU RENDEZ-VOUS DES TERRE-NEUVAS. Paris: Fayard, 1931. 249p.

________. Paris: Fayard, 1936. 249p. (Collection "Les Enquêtes du Commissaire Maigret")

________. Paris: Fayard, 1954. 222p.

________. Paris: Fayard, 1956. 218p. (Collection "Le Commissaire Maigret")

________. In an untitled collection with LE CHARRETIER DE LA "PROVIDENCE" and PIETR-LE-LETTON. Paris: Fayard, 1956. ("Bibliothèque Simenon," 2)

________. Paris: Fayard, 1964. 219p. (Collection "Le Commissaire Maigret")

________. Paris: Librairie Générale Française, 1972. 187p. (Le Livre de poche, 2972)

English Translations
British Editions

THE SAILOR'S RENDEZVOUS. In MAIGRET KEEPS A RENDEZVOUS, tr. by Margaret Ludwig. London: George Routledge and Son, 1940. vi, 287p. (Also includes THE SAINT FIACRE AFFAIR)

________. In MAIGRET KEEPS A RENDEZVOUS, tr. by Margaret Ludwig. London: Routledge and Kegan Paul, 1948. 287p. (Also includes THE SAINT FIACRE AFFAIR)

________, tr. by Margaret Ludwig. Harmondsworth, Baltimore: Penguin, 1970. 127p. (paper)

American Editions

________. In MAIGRET KEEPS A RENDEZVOUS, tr. by Margaret Ludwig. New York: Harcourt, Brace & World, 1941. vi, 312p. (Also includes THE SAINT FIACRE AFFAIR)

2. LE CHARRETIER DE LA "PROVIDENCE." Paris: Fayard, 1931. 250p.

________. Paris: Fayard, 1936. 250p. (Collection "Les Enquêtes du Commissaire Maigret," 3)

________. In an untitled collection with PIETR-LE-LETTON and AU RENDEZ-VOUS DES TERRE-NEUVAS. Paris: Fayard, ("Bibliothèque Simenon," 2)

________. Paris: Fayard, 1956. 254p. (Collection "Le Commissaire Maigret")

________. Paris: Librairie Générale Française, 1970. 160p. (Le Livre de poche, 2907)

English Translations
British Editions

THE CRIME AT LOCK 14. In THE TRIUMPH OF INSPECTOR MAIGRET. (no translator). London: Hurst and Blackett, 1934. 288p. (Also includes THE SHADOW ON THE COURTYARD)

MAIGRET MEETS A MILORD, tr. by Robert Baldick. Harmondsworth, Baltimore: Penguin, 1963. 123p. (paper)

American Editions

THE CRIME AT LOCK 14, bound with THE SHADOW ON THE COURTYARD. (no translator). New York: Covici, Friede; Toronto: McLeod, 1934. 317p.

3. LE CHIEN JAUNE. Paris: Fayard, 1931. 249p.

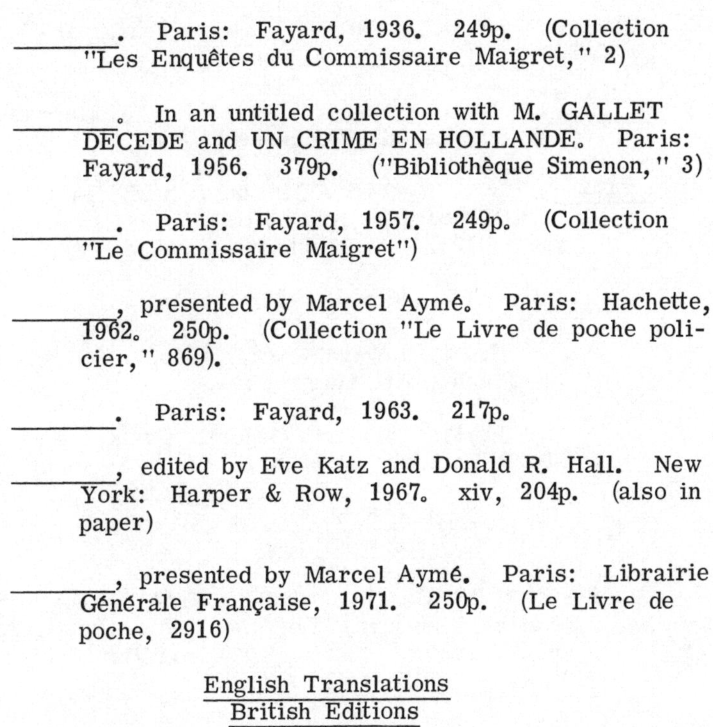

________. Paris: Fayard, 1936. 249p. (Collection "Les Enquêtes du Commissaire Maigret," 2)

________. In an untitled collection with M. GALLET DECEDE and UN CRIME EN HOLLANDE. Paris: Fayard, 1956. 379p. ("Bibliothèque Simenon," 3)

________. Paris: Fayard, 1957. 249p. (Collection "Le Commissaire Maigret")

________, presented by Marcel Aymé. Paris: Hachette, 1962. 250p. (Collection "Le Livre de poche policier," 869).

________. Paris: Fayard, 1963. 217p.

________, edited by Eve Katz and Donald R. Hall. New York: Harper & Row, 1967. xiv, 204p. (also in paper)

________, presented by Marcel Aymé. Paris: Librairie Générale Française, 1971. 250p. (Le Livre de poche, 2916)

English Translations
British Editions

A FACE FOR A CLUE. In PATIENCE OF MAIGRET, tr. by Geoffrey Sainsbury. London: George Routledge & Sons; Toronto: Musson, 1939. vi, 319p. (Also includes A BATTLE OF NERVES)

________ bound with A CRIME IN HOLLAND and tr. by Geoffrey Sainsbury. Harmondsworth: Penguin Books, 1952. 283p. (paper)

American Editions

________. In PATIENCE OF MAIGRET, tr. by Geoffrey Sainsbury. New York: Harcourt, Brace & Co., 1940. 311p. (Also includes A BATTLE OF NERVES)

________. In PATIENCE OF MAIGRET, tr. by Geoffrey Sainsbury. New York: World Publishers, 1943. 317p. (paper) (Also includes A BATTLE OF NERVES)

4. UN CRIME EN HOLLANDE. Paris: Fayard, 1931. 249p.

________. Paris: Fayard, 1936. 249p. (Collection "Les Enquêtes du Commissaire Maigret," 4)

________. In an untitled collection with M. GALLET DECEDE and LE CHIEN JAUNE. Paris: Fayard, 1956. 379p. ("Bibliothèque Simenon," 3)

________. Paris: Fayard, 1959. 254p.

________. Paris: Fayard, 1962. 254p. (Collection "Le Commissaire Maigret")

________. Paris: Librairie Générale Française, 1971. 185p. (Le Livre de poche, 2917)

<u>English Translations</u>
<u>British Editions</u>

A CRIME IN HOLLAND. In MAIGRET ABROAD, tr. by Geoffrey Sainsbury. London: George Routledge & Sons; Toronto: Musson, 1940. vi 312p. (Also includes AT THE "GAI-MOULIN")

________ bound with A FACE FOR A CLUE and tr. by Geoffrey Sainsbury. Harmondsworth: Penguin Books, 1952. 283p. (paper)

<u>American Editions</u>

________. In MAIGRET ABROAD, tr. by Geoffrey Sainsbury. New York: Harcourt, Brace & Co., 1940. 315p. (Also includes AT THE "GAI-MOULIN")

5. LA DANSEUSE DU GAI-MOULIN. Paris: Fayard, 1931. 252p.

________. Paris: Fayard, 1956. 223p.

________. Paris: Fayard, 1957. 223p.

________. In an untitled collection with MAIGRET and LE FOU DE BERGERAC. Paris: Fayard, 1959. 347p. ("Bibliothèque Simenon," 8)

_______. Paris: Librairie Générale Française, 1971. 190p. (Le Livre de poche, 2920)

English Translations
British Editions

AT THE "GAI-MOULIN." In MAIGRET ABROAD, tr. by Geoffrey Sainsbury. London: George Routledge & Sons; Toronto: Musson, 1940. vi 312p. (Also includes A CRIME IN HOLLAND)

_______ bound with A BATTLE OF NERVES and tr. by Geoffrey Sainsbury. Harmondsworth: Penguin Books, 1950. 286p. (paper)

_______ bound with A BATTLE OF NERVES and tr. by Geoffrey Sainsbury. Harmondsworth: Penguin Books, 1951. 286p. (paper: a reissue)

American Editions

_______. In MAIGRET ABROAD, tr. by Geoffrey Sainsbury. New York: Harcourt, Brace & Co., 1940. 315p. (Also includes A CRIME IN HOLLAND)

6. M. GALLET DECEDE. Paris: Fayard, 1931. 253p.

_______. Paris: Fayard, 1932. 219p.

_______. Paris: Fayard, 1936. 249p. (Collection "Les Enquêtes du Commissaire Maigret," 9)

_______. Paris: Fayard, 1952. 253p.

_______. In an untitled collection with UN CRIME EN HOLLANDE and LE CHIEN JAUNE. Paris: Fayard, 1956. 379p.

_______. Paris: Fayard, 1957. 249p. (Collection "Le Commissaire Maigret")

_______. Paris: Librairie Générale Française, 1971. 188p. (Le Livre de poche, 2914)

English Translations
British Editions

THE DEATH OF M. GALLET. In INTRODUCING INSPECTOR MAIGRET, tr. by Anthony Abbott. London: Hurst and Blackett, 1933. 288p. (Also includes THE CRIME OF INSPECTOR OF MAIGRET)

________. In INTRODUCING INSPECTOR MAIGRET, tr. by Anthony Abbott. London: Hurst and Blackett, 1938. 255p. (cheaper edition) (Also includes THE CRIME OF INSPECTOR MAIGRET)

MAIGRET STONEWALLED, tr. by Margaret Marshall. Harmondsworth, Baltimore: Penguin Books, 1963. 135p. (paper)

American Editions

THE DEATH OF MONSIEUR GALLET. (no translator). New York: Covici, Friede, 1932. 262p.

7. LA NUIT DU CARREFOUR. Paris: Fayard, 1931. 251p.

________, ed. by P. W. Packer. Adapted from the complete edition. London: Oxford University Press, 1935. 63p. (also in paper) (Rapid Reading French Texts)

________. Paris: Fayard, 1936. 251p. (Collection "Les Enquêtes du Commissaire Maigret," 8)

________. In an untitled collection with L'OMBRE CHINOISE and LA GUINGUETTE A DEUX SOUS. Paris: Fayard, 1956. 380p. ("Bibliothèque Simenon," 1)

________. Paris: Fayard, 1957. 251p. (Collection "Le Commissaire Maigret")

________. Paris: Librairie Générale Française, 1970. 159p. (Le Livre de poche, 2908)

________; une enquête de Maigret. With an introduction

by Albert Demazière. Geneva: Editions de Crémille Baauval, 1972. 241p. (Collection "Les Grands maîtres du roman policier")

English Translations
British Editions

THE CROSSROAD MURDERS. In INSPECTOR MAIGRET INVESTIGATES, tr. by Anthony Abbott. London: Hurst and Blackett, 1933. 288p. (Also includes THE CASE OF PETER THE LETT)

MAIGRET AT THE CROSSROADS, tr. by Robert Baldeck. Harmondsworth: Penguin Books, 1963. 135p. (paper)

American Editions

THE CROSSROAD MURDERS. (No translator). New York: Covici, Friede, 1933. 240p.

8. LE PENDU DE SAINT-PHOLIEN. Paris: Fayard, 1931. 249p.

________. Paris: Fayard, 1936. 249p. (Collection "Les Enquêtes du Commissaire Maigret," 11)

________. In an untitled collection with LE PORT DES BRUMES and L'ECLUSE NO. 1. Paris: Fayard, 1956. 380p. ("Bibliothèque Simenon," 4)

________. Paris: Fayard, 1962. 222p. (Collection "Le Commissaire Maigret")

MAIGRET ET LE PENDU DE SAINT PHOLIEN, ed. by Geoffrey Goodall. New York: St. Martin's Press, London: Macmillan, 1965. vi, 161p.

LE PENDU DE SAINT-PHOLIEN. Paris: Librairie Générale Française, 1972. 188p. (Le Livre de poche, 2921)

English Translations
British Editions

THE CRIME OF INSPECTOR MAIGRET. In INTRODUC-

ING INSPECTOR MAIGRET, tr. by Anthony Abbott. London: Hurst and Blackett, 1933. 288p. (Also includes THE DEATH OF M. GALLET)

________. In INTRODUCING INSPECTOR MAIGRET, tr. by Anthony Abbott. London: Hurst and Blackett, 1938. 255p. (cheaper edition). (Also includes THE DEATH OF M. GALLET)

MAIGRET AND THE HUNDRED GIBBETS, tr. by Tony White. Harmondsworth, Baltimore: Penguin Books, 1963. 122p. (paper)

American Editions

THE CRIME OF INSPECTOR MAIGRET, tr. by Anthony Abbott. New York: Covici, Friede, 1933. 244p.

9. PIETR-LE-LETTON. Paris: Fayard, 1931. 251p.

________. Paris: Fayard, 1936. 251p. (Collection "Les Enquêtes du Commissaire Maigret," 7)

________. In an untitled collection with LE CHARRETIER DE LA "PROVIDENCE" and AU RENDEZ-VOUS DES TERRE-NUEVAS. Paris: Fayard, 1956. ("Bibliothèque Simenon," 2)

________. Paris: Fayard, 1959. 251p. (Collection "Le Commissaire Maigret")

________. Paris: Fayard, 1962. 222p.

________. Paris: Libraire Générale Française, 1970. 220p. (Le Livre de poche, 2909)

English Translations
British Editions

THE CASE OF PETER THE LETT. In INSPECTOR MAIGRET INVESTIGATES, tr. by Anthony Abbott. London: Hurst and Blackett, 1933. 288p. (Also includes THE CROSSROAD MURDERS)

________. In INSPECTOR MAIGRET INVESTIGATES, tr. by Anthony Abbott. London: Hurst and Blackett, 1933. 288p. (cheaper edition). (Also includes THE CROSSROAD MURDERS)

MAIGRET AND THE ENIGMATIC LETT, tr. by Daphne Woodward. Harmondsworth, Baltimore: Penguin Books, 1963. 139p. (paper)

American Editions

THE STRANGE CASE OF PETER THE LETT. (no translator). New York: Covici, Friede, 1933. vi, 267p.

10. LE RELAIS D'ALSACE. Paris: Fayard, 1931. 252p.

________. Paris: Fayard, 1952. 254p.

________. Paris: Fayard, 1957. 252p.

________. In an untitled collection with LA TETE D'UN HOMME and LA MAISON DU CANAL. Paris: Fayard, 1957. 366p. ("Bibliothèque Simenon," 6)

________. Paris: Librairie Générale Française, 1971. 187p. (Le Livre de poche, 2918)

English Translations
British Editions

THE MAN FROM EVERYWHERE. In MAIGRET AND M. L'ABBE, tr. by Stuart Gilbert. London: George Routledge and Sons, 1941. 311p. (Also includes DEATH OF A HARBOUR MASTER)

________ bound with NEWHAVEN-DIEPPE and tr. by Stuart Gilbert. Harmondsworth: Penguin Books, 1952. 252p. (paper)

American Editions

________. In MAIGRET AND M. L'ABBE, tr. by Stuart Gilbert. New York: Harcourt, Brace & Co., 1942. vi, 312p. (Also includes DEATH OF A HARBOR MASTER)

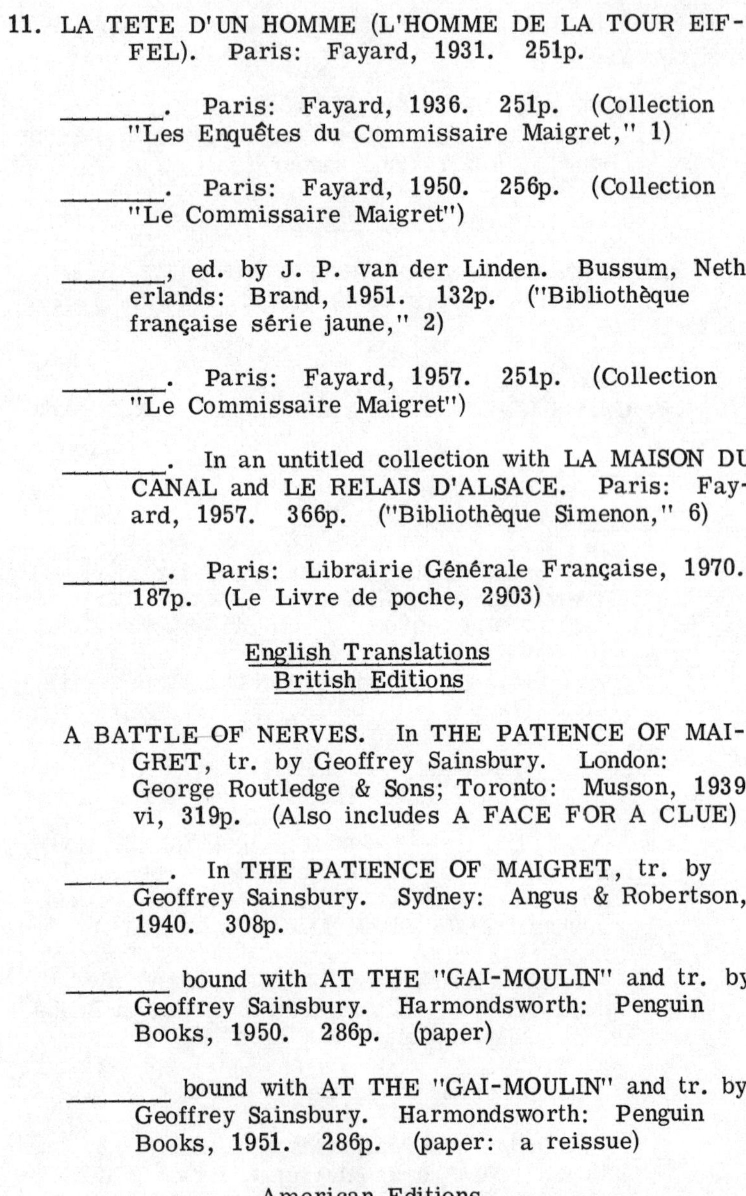

11. LA TETE D'UN HOMME (L'HOMME DE LA TOUR EIFFEL). Paris: Fayard, 1931. 251p.

________. Paris: Fayard, 1936. 251p. (Collection "Les Enquêtes du Commissaire Maigret," 1)

________. Paris: Fayard, 1950. 256p. (Collection "Le Commissaire Maigret")

________, ed. by J. P. van der Linden. Bussum, Netherlands: Brand, 1951. 132p. ("Bibliothèque française série jaune," 2)

________. Paris: Fayard, 1957. 251p. (Collection "Le Commissaire Maigret")

________. In an untitled collection with LA MAISON DU CANAL and LE RELAIS D'ALSACE. Paris: Fayard, 1957. 366p. ("Bibliothèque Simenon," 6)

________. Paris: Librairie Générale Française, 1970. 187p. (Le Livre de poche, 2903)

English Translations
British Editions

A BATTLE OF NERVES. In THE PATIENCE OF MAIGRET, tr. by Geoffrey Sainsbury. London: George Routledge & Sons; Toronto: Musson, 1939. vi, 319p. (Also includes A FACE FOR A CLUE)

________. In THE PATIENCE OF MAIGRET, tr. by Geoffrey Sainsbury. Sydney: Angus & Robertson, 1940. 308p.

________ bound with AT THE "GAI-MOULIN" and tr. by Geoffrey Sainsbury. Harmondsworth: Penguin Books, 1950. 286p. (paper)

________ bound with AT THE "GAI-MOULIN" and tr. by Geoffrey Sainsbury. Harmondsworth: Penguin Books, 1951. 286p. (paper: a reissue)

American Editions

________. In THE PATIENCE OF MAIGRET, tr. by Geoffrey Sainsbury. New York: Harcourt, Brace

& Co., 1940. 311p. (Also includes A FACE FOR A CLUE)

_______. In THE PATIENCE OF MAIGRET, tr. by Geoffrey Sainsbury. New York: World Publisher, 1943. 317p. (paper) (Also includes A FACE FOR A CLUE)

1932

12. L'AFFAIRE SAINT FIACRE. Paris: Fayard, 1932. 251p.

_______. Paris: Fayard, 1955. 224p.

_______. Paris: Fayard, 1957. 223p. (Collection "Le Commissaire Maigret")

_______. In an untitled collection with CHEZ LES FLAMANDS and "LIBERTY BAR." Paris: Fayard, 1957. 348p. ("Bibliothèque Simenon," 5)

_______. Paris: Librairie Générale Française, 1970. 189p. (Le Livre de poche, 2904)

_______, adapted into easy French by Charles Milou. Paris: Hachette, 1973. 71p. (Collection "Textes en français facile--Série récits")

English Translations
British Editions

THE SAINT-FIACRE AFFAIR. In MAIGRET KEEPS A RENDEZVOUS, tr. by Margaret Ludwig. George Routledge & Sons, 1940. vi, 287p. (Also includes THE SAILOR'S RENDEZVOUS)

_______. In MAIGRET KEEPS A RENDEZVOUS, tr. by Margaret Ludwig. George Routledge & Sons, 1948. 287p. (cheaper edition). (Also includes THE SAILOR'S RENDEZVOUS)

_______. In MAIGRET KEEPS A RENDEZVOUS, tr. by Margaret Ludwig. Routledge & Kegan Paul, 1951. 287p. (cheaper edition) (Also includes THE SAILOR'S RENDEZVOUS)

MAIGRET GOES HOME, tr. by Robert Baldick. Harmondsworth: Penguin Books, 1967. 139p. (paper)

American Editions

THE SAINT-FIACRE AFFAIR. In MAIGRET KEEPS A RENDEZVOUS, tr. by Margaret Ludwig. New York: Harcourt, Brace & Co., 1941. vi, 312p. (Also includes THE SAILOR'S RENDEZVOUS)

MAIGRET GOES HOME, tr. by Robert Baldick. Baltimore: Penguin Books, 1967. 138p. (paper)

13. CHEZ LES FLAMANDS. Paris: Fayard, 1932. 250p.

________. Paris: Fayard, 1954. 223p.

________. Paris: Fayard, 1957. 219p. (Collection "Le Commissaire Maigret")

________. In an untitled collection with "LIBERTY BAR" and L'AFFAIRE SAINT FIACRE. Paris: Fayard, 1957. 348p. ("Bibliothèque Simenon," 5)

________. Paris: Librairie Générale Française, 1973. 188p. (Le Livre de poche, 2927)

English Translations
British Editions

THE FLEMISH SHOP. In MAIGRET TO THE RESCUE, tr. by Geoffrey Sainsbury. London: George Routledge & Sons; Toronto: Musson, 1940. vi, 285p. (Also includes GUINGUETTE BY THE SEINE)

________. In MAIGRET TO THE RESCUE, tr. by Geoffrey Sainsbury. London: Routledge & Kegan Paul, 1948. vi, 285p. (cheaper edition). (Also includes GUINGUETTE BY THE SEINE)

________. In MAIGRET TO THE RESCUE, tr. by Geoffrey Sainsbury. London: Pan Books, 1950. 221p. (paper) (Also includes GUINGUETTE BY THE SEINE)

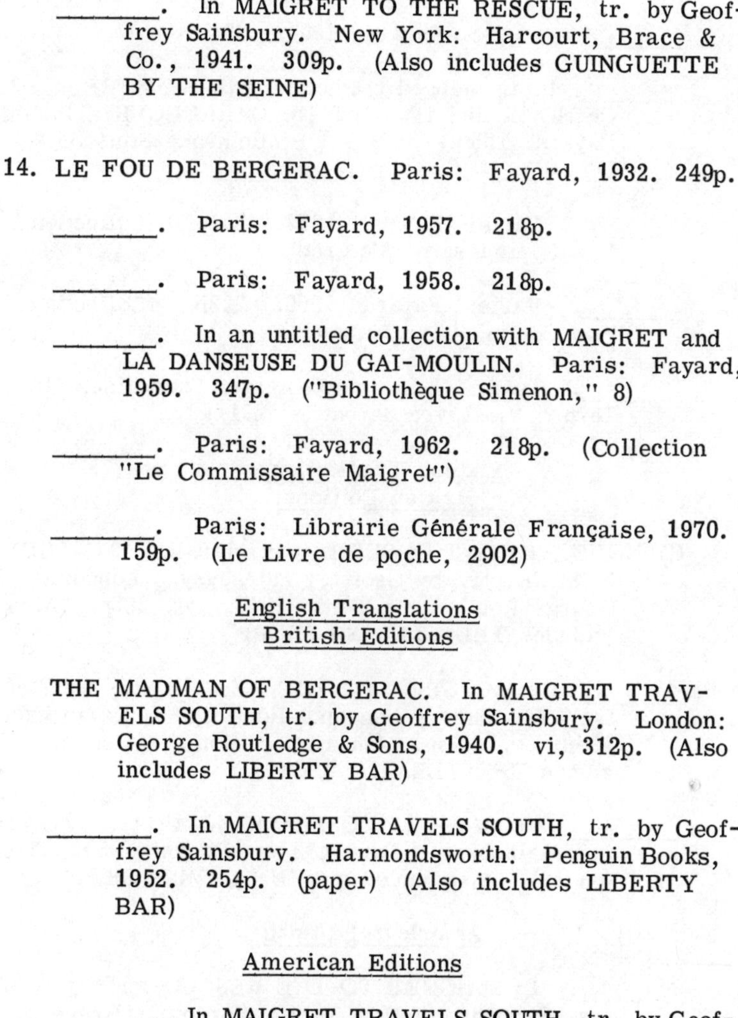

American Editions

________. In MAIGRET TO THE RESCUE, tr. by Geoffrey Sainsbury. New York: Harcourt, Brace & Co., 1941. 309p. (Also includes GUINGUETTE BY THE SEINE)

14. LE FOU DE BERGERAC. Paris: Fayard, 1932. 249p.

________. Paris: Fayard, 1957. 218p.

________. Paris: Fayard, 1958. 218p.

________. In an untitled collection with MAIGRET and LA DANSEUSE DU GAI-MOULIN. Paris: Fayard, 1959. 347p. ("Bibliothèque Simenon," 8)

________. Paris: Fayard, 1962. 218p. (Collection "Le Commissaire Maigret")

________. Paris: Librairie Générale Française, 1970. 159p. (Le Livre de poche, 2902)

English Translations
British Editions

THE MADMAN OF BERGERAC. In MAIGRET TRAVELS SOUTH, tr. by Geoffrey Sainsbury. London: George Routledge & Sons, 1940. vi, 312p. (Also includes LIBERTY BAR)

________. In MAIGRET TRAVELS SOUTH, tr. by Geoffrey Sainsbury. Harmondsworth: Penguin Books, 1952. 254p. (paper) (Also includes LIBERTY BAR)

American Editions

________. In MAIGRET TRAVELS SOUTH, tr. by Geoffrey Sainsbury. New York: Harcourt, Brace & Co., 1940. (Also includes LIBERTY BAR)

________. In MAIGRET TRAVELS SOUTH, tr. by Geoffrey Sainsbury. New York: World, 1944. 308p. (paper) (Also includes LIBERTY BAR)

15. LA GUINGUETTE A DEUX SOUS. Paris: Fayard, 1932. 252p.

________. Paris: Fayard, 1954. 224p.

________, In an untitled collection with L'OMBRE CHINOISE and LA NUIT DU CARREFOUR. Paris: Fayard, 1956. 380p. ("Bibliothèque Simenon," 1)

________. Paris: Fayard, 1957. 251p. (Collection "Le Commissaire Maigret")

________. Paris: Fayard, 1959. 223p. (Collection "Le Commissaire Maigret")

________. Paris: Librairie Générale Française, 1971. 187p. (Le Livre de poche, 2911)

English Translations
British Editions

GUINGUETTE BY THE SEINE. In MAIGRET TO THE RESCUE, tr. by Geoffrey Sainsbury. London: George Routledge & Sons, 1940. vi, 285p. (Also includes THE FLEMISH SHOP)

________. In MAIGRET TO THE RESCUE, tr. by Geoffrey Sainsbury. London: Routledge & Kegan Paul, 1948. vi, 285p. (cheaper edition). (Also includes THE FLEMISH SHOP)

________. In MAIGRET TO THE RESCUE, tr. by Geoffrey Sainsbury. London: Pan Books, 1950. 221p. (paper) (Also includes THE FLEMISH SHOP)

American Editions

________. In MAIGRET TO THE RESCUE, tr. by Geoffrey Sainsbury. New York: Harcourt, Brace & Co., 1941. 309p. (Also includes THE FLEMISH SHOP)

16. "LIBERTY BAR." Paris: Fayard, 1932. 254p.

________. Paris: Fayard, 1936. 254p. (Collection

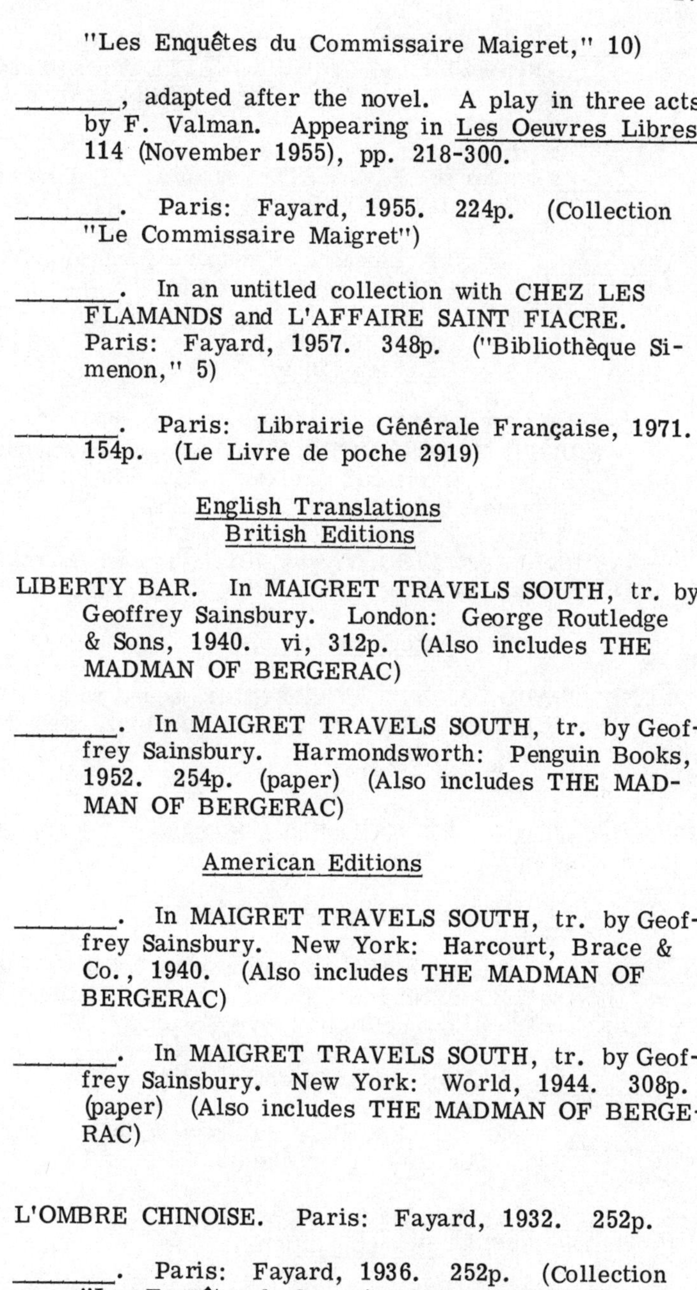

"Les Enquêtes du Commissaire Maigret," 10)

________, adapted after the novel. A play in three acts by F. Valman. Appearing in Les Oeuvres Libres 114 (November 1955), pp. 218-300.

________. Paris: Fayard, 1955. 224p. (Collection "Le Commissaire Maigret")

________. In an untitled collection with CHEZ LES FLAMANDS and L'AFFAIRE SAINT FIACRE. Paris: Fayard, 1957. 348p. ("Bibliothèque Simenon," 5)

________. Paris: Librairie Générale Française, 1971. 154p. (Le Livre de poche 2919)

English Translations
British Editions

LIBERTY BAR. In MAIGRET TRAVELS SOUTH, tr. by Geoffrey Sainsbury. London: George Routledge & Sons, 1940. vi, 312p. (Also includes THE MADMAN OF BERGERAC)

________. In MAIGRET TRAVELS SOUTH, tr. by Geoffrey Sainsbury. Harmondsworth: Penguin Books, 1952. 254p. (paper) (Also includes THE MADMAN OF BERGERAC)

American Editions

________. In MAIGRET TRAVELS SOUTH, tr. by Geoffrey Sainsbury. New York: Harcourt, Brace & Co., 1940. (Also includes THE MADMAN OF BERGERAC)

________. In MAIGRET TRAVELS SOUTH, tr. by Geoffrey Sainsbury. New York: World, 1944. 308p. (paper) (Also includes THE MADMAN OF BERGERAC)

17. L'OMBRE CHINOISE. Paris: Fayard, 1932. 252p.

________. Paris: Fayard, 1936. 252p. (Collection "Les Enquêtes du Commissaire Maigret," 6)

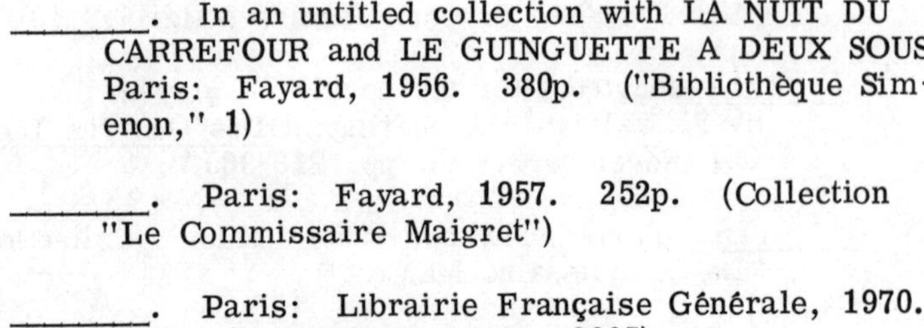

________. In an untitled collection with LA NUIT DU CARREFOUR and LE GUINGUETTE A DEUX SOUS. Paris: Fayard, 1956. 380p. ("Bibliothèque Simenon," 1)

________. Paris: Fayard, 1957. 252p. (Collection "Le Commissaire Maigret")

________. Paris: Librairie Française Générale, 1970. 157p. (Le Livre de poche, 2905)

English Translations
British Editions

THE SHADOW ON THE COURTYARD. In THE TRIUMPH OF INSPECTOR MAIGRET. (no translator). London: Hurst and Blackett, 1934. 288p. (Also includes THE CRIME AT LOCK 14)

MAIGRET MYSTIFIED, tr. by Jean Stewart. Harmondsworth: Penguin Books, 1965. 138p. (paper)

American Editions

THE SHADOW IN THE COURTYARD, bound with THE CRIME AT LOCK 14. (no translator). New York: Covici, Friede, 1934. 317p.

18. LE PASSAGER DU "POLARLYS." Paris: Fayard, 1932. 249p.

________. Paris: Fayard, 1954. 222p.

________. In an untitled collection with LE HAUT-MAL and LES GENS D'EN FACE. Paris: Fayard, 1961. 319p. ("Bibliothèque Simenon," 9)

________. Paris: Fayard, 1965. 222p.

________. Paris: Librairie Française Générale, 1971. 188p. (Le Livre de poche, 2915)

English Translations
British Editions

THE MYSTERY OF THE "POLARLYS." In TWO LATI-

TUDES, tr. by Stuart Gilbert. London: George Routledge & Sons; Toronto: Musson, 1942. 320p. (Also includes TROPIC MOON)

_______. In IN TWO LATITUDES, tr. Stuart Gilbert. Harmondsworth: Penguin Books, 1952. 320p. (paper)

American Editions

DANGER AT SEA. In ON LAND AND SEA, tr. by Victor Kosta. Garden City, N.Y.: Hanover House, 1954. (Also includes DANGER ASHORE)

19. LE PORT DES BRUMES. Paris: Fayard, 1932. 250p.

_______. Paris: Fayard, 1936. 250p. (Collection "Les Enquêtes du Commissaire Maigret," 5)

_______. In an untitled collection with L'ECLUSE NO. 1 and LE PENDU DE SAINT PHOLIEN. Paris: Fayard, 1956. 380p. ("Bibliothèque Simenon," 4)

_______. Paris: Fayard, 1957. 250p. (Collection "Le Commissaire Maigret")

_______. Paris: Librairie Générale Française, 1972. 220p. (Le Livre de poche, 2924)

English Translations
British Editions

DEATH OF A HARBOUR MASTER. In MAIGRET AND M. L'ABBE, tr. by Stuart Gilbert. London: George Routledge & Sons, 1941. 311p. (Also includes THE MAN FROM EVERYWHERE)

American Editions

DEATH OF A HARBOR MASTER. In MAIGRET AND M. L'ABBE, tr. by Stuart Gilbert. New York: Harcourt, Brace & Co., 1942. vi, 312p. (Also includes THE MAN FROM EVERYWHERE)

20. LES TREIZE COUPABLES. Paris: Fayard, 1932. 250p.

________. Paris: Fayard, 1957. 222p. (Collection "Le Commissaire Maigret")

________. In an untitled collection with LES TREIZE MYSTERES and LES TREIZE ENIGMES. Paris: Fayard, 1958. 316p. ("Bibliothèque Simenon," 7)

________. Paris: Fayard, 1966, 222p.

________. Paris: Librairie Générale Française, 1973. 179p. (Le Livre de poche, 3713)

21. LES TREIZE ENIGMES. Paris: Fayard, 1932. 252p.

________. Paris: Fayard, 1958. 189p.

________. In an untitled collection with LES TREIZE COUPABLES and LES TREIZE MYSTERES. Paris: Fayard, 1958. 316p. ("Bibliothèque Simenon," 7)

________. Paris: Fayard, 1966. 189p.

________. Paris: Librairie Générale Française, 1973. 158p. (Le Livre de poche, 2929)

22. LES TREIZE MYSTERES. Paris: Fayard, 1932. 253p.

________. Paris: Fayard, 1958. 217p.

________. In an untitled collection with LES TREIZE COUPABLES and LES TREIZE ENIGMES. Paris: Fayard, 1958. 316p. ("Bibliothèque Simenon," 7)

________. Paris: Fayard, 1965. 217p.

________. Paris: Librairie Générale Française, 1973. 150p. (Le Livre de poche, 2930)

1933

23. L'ANE ROUGE. Paris: Fayard, 1933. 253p.

________. Paris: Fayard, 1956. 224p.

_______. Paris: Fayard, 1957. 222p.

_______. Paris: Fayard, 1958. 222p.

_______. In an untitled collection with LES FIANÇAILLES DE MR. HIRE and LE COUP DE LUNE. Paris: Fayard, 1961. 316p. ("Bibliothèque Simenon," 10)

_______. Paris: Librairie Générale Française, 1972. 187p. (Le Livre de poche, 2926)

24. LE COUP DE LUNE. Paris: Fayard, 1933. 252p.

_______. Paris: Fayard, 1953. 221p.

_______. Paris: Fayard, 1956. 221p.

_______. With an introduction by Gilbert Sigaux. Paris: Club Français du Livre, 1955. viii, 248p.

_______. In an untitled collection with LES FIANÇAILLES DE MR. HIRE and L'ANE ROUGE. Paris: Fayard, 1961. 316p. ("Bibliothèque Simenon," 10)

_______. With an introduction by André Parinaud. Paris: Club des Amis du Livre, (no date). 286p.

_______. Paris: Librairie Générale Française, 1970. 221p. (Le Livre de poche, 2906)

English Translations
British Editions

TROPIC MOON. In TWO LATITUDES, tr. by Stuart Gilbert. London: George Routledge & Sons; Toronto: Musson, 1942. vi, 280p. (Also includes THE MYSTERY OF THE "POLARLYS")

_______. In IN TWO LATITUDES, tr. by Stuart Gilbert. Harmondsworth: Penguin Books, 1952. 320p. (paper) (Also includes THE MYSTERY OF THE "POLARLYS")

American Editions

________, tr. by Stuart Gilbert. New York: Harcourt, Brace & Co., 1943. 218p.

25. L'ECLUSE NO. 1. Paris: Fayard, 1933. 252p.

________. Paris: Fayard, 1955. 224p.

________. Paris: Presses de la Cite. 224p.

________. In an untitled collection with LE PENDU DE SAINT PHOLIEN and LE PORT DES BRUMES. Paris: Fayard, 1956. 380p. ("Bibliothèque Simenon," 4)

________. Paris: Fayard, 1957. 223p. (Collection "Le Commissaire Maigret")

________. Paris: Librairie Générale Française, 1972. 158p. (Le Livre de poche, 2923)

English Translations
British Editions

THE LOCK AT CHARENTON. In MAIGRET SITS IT OUT, tr. by Margaret Ludwig. London: George Routledge & Sons; Toronto: Musson, 1941. 275p. (Also includes MAIGRET RETURNS)

________. In MAIGRET SITS IT OUT, tr. by Margaret Ludwig. Harmondsworth: Penguin Books, 1952. (paper) (Also includes MAIGRET RETURNS)

American Editions

________. In MAIGRET SITS IT OUT, tr. by Margaret Ludwig. New York: Harcourt, Brace & Co., 1941. 305p. (Also includes MAIGRET RETURNS)

26. LES FIANÇAILLES DE MR. HIRE. Paris: Fayard, 1933. 249p.

________. Paris: Fayard, 1957. 224p. (Collection "Le Commissaire Maigret")

________. In an untitled collection with L'ANE ROUGE and LE COUP DE LUNE. Paris: ("Bibliothèque Simenon," 10)

________. Paris: Fayard, 1966. 222p.

________. Paris: Librairie Générale Française, 1970. 160p. (Le Livre de poche, 2900)

English Translations
British Editions

MR. HIRE'S ENGAGEMENT, tr. by Daphne Woodward. In THE SACRIFICE. London: Hamish Hamilton, 1956. 254p. (Also includes YOUNG CARDINAUD, tr. by Richard Brain)

________, tr. by Daphne Woodward. In THE SACRIFICE. London: Hamish Hamilton, 1958. 256p. (cheaper edition). (Also includes YOUNG CARDINAUD, tr. by Richard Brain)

________, tr. by Daphne Woodward. London: Hutchinson, 1958. 192p. (paper)

________, tr. by Daphne Woodward. In a collection entitled A SIMENON OMNIBUS. London: Hamish Hamilton, 1965. 503p. (Also includes THE MAN FROM ARCHANGEL, IN CASE OF EMERGENCY, SUNDAY and THE PREMIER)

27. LES GENS D'EN FACE. Paris: Fayard, 1933. 251p.

________. Appearing in series in Annales Politiques et Littéraires, 101 (September 1-October 13, 1933): pp. 255-60, 284-9, 313-17, 340-5, 369-73, 398-402, 425-8.

________. Paris: Fayard, 1957. 222p. (Collection "Le Commissaire Maigret")

________. Paris: Fayard, 1960. 221p.

________. In an untitled collection with LE HAUT-MAL and LE PASSAGER DU "POLARLYS." Paris: Fayard, 1961. 319p. ("Bibliothèque Simenon," 9)

________. Paris: Librairie Générale Française, 1971. 217p. (Le Livre de poche, 2912)

English Translations
British Editions

THE WINDOW OVER THE WAY, bound with THE GENDARME'S REPORT and tr. by Geoffrey Sainsbury. London: Routledge and Kegan Paul; New York: British Book Service, 1951. 291p.

________, tr. by Robert Baldick. Harmondsworth: Penguin Books, 1966. 137p. (paper)

________, tr. by Robert Baldick. Harmondsworth: Penguin Books, 1972. 138p. (paper)

American Editions

DANGER ASHORE. In ON LAND AND SEA, tr. by Victor Kosta. Garden City, N.Y.: Hanover House, 1954. (Also includes DANGER AT SEA)

28. LE HAUT-MAL. Paris: Fayard, 1933. (no price)

________. Illustrated by Watrin. Paris: Calmann-Lévy, 1947. 237p. (limited issues on finer paper)

________. Paris: Fayard, 1956. 223p.

________. Paris: Fayard, 1958. 222p.

________. In an untitled collection with LES GENS D'EN FACE and LE PASSAGER DU "POLARLYS." Paris: Fayard, 1961. 319p. ("Bibliothèque Simenon," 9)

________. Paris: Librairie Générale Française, 1972. (Le Livre de poche, 2925)

English Translations
British Editions

THE WOMAN IN THE GREY HOUSE. In AFFAIRS OF DESTINY, tr. by Stuart Gilbert. London: George Routledge & Sons; Toronto: Musson, 1942. 255p. (Also includes NEWHAVEN-DIEPPE)

________. In AFFAIRS OF DESTINY, tr. by Stuart Gilbert. London: George Routledge & Sons, 1948. 255p. (cheaper edition)

________, tr. by Stuart Gilbert. London: Brown & Watson, 1958. 157p.

________, tr. by Stuart Gilbert. London: Brown & Watson, 1962. 156p.

American Editions

THE WOMAN IN THE GRAY HOUSE. In AFFAIRS OF DESTINY, tr. by Stuart Gilbert. New York: Harcourt, Brace & Co., 1944. 265p. (Also includes NEWHAVEN-DIEPPE)

29. LA MAISON DU CANAL. Paris: Fayard, 1933. 252p.

________. Paris: Calmann-Lévy, 1947. 252p.

________. Paris: Fayard, 1956. 252p.

________. In an untitled collection with LA TETE D'UN HOMME and LE RELAIS D'ALSACE. Paris: Fayard, 1957. 366p. ("Bibliothèque Simenon," 6)

________. Paris: Fayard, 1958. 252p.

________. Lausanne: La Guilde du Livre, 1959. 212p. (Collection "La Guilde du Livre," 339)

________. Paris: Librairie Générale Française, 1970. 190p. (Le Livre de poche, 2901)

English Translations
British Editions

THE HOUSE BY THE CANAL, bound with THE OSTENDERS and tr. by Geoffrey Sainsbury. London: Routledge & Kegan Paul, 1952. 266p.

________, bound with THE OSTENDERS and tr. by Geoffrey Sainsbury. London: Routledge & Kegan Paul, 1955. 268p. (cheaper edition)

1934

30. L'HOMME DE LONDRES. Paris: Fayard, 1934.

_______. Paris: Fayard, 1948.

_______. Paris: Fayard, 1962. 221p.

_______. Paris: Librairie Générale Française, 1971. 187p. (Le Livre de poche, 2913)

English Translations
British Editions

NEWHAVEN-DIEPPE. In AFFAIRS OF DESTINY, tr. by Stuart Gilbert. London: George Routledge & Sons; Toronto: Musson, 1942. 255p. (Also includes THE WOMAN IN THE GREY HOUSE)

_______. In AFFAIRS OF DESTINY, tr. by Stuart Gilbert. London: George Routledge & Sons, 1948. 255p. (cheaper edition). (Also includes THE WOMAN IN THE GREY HOUSE)

_______, bound with THE MAN FROM EVERYWHERE and tr. by Stuart Gilbert. Harmondsworth: Penguin Books, 1952. 252p. (paper)

American Editions

_______. In AFFAIRS OF DESTINY, tr. by Stuart Gilbert. New York: Harcourt, Brace & Co., 1944. 265p. (Also includes THE WOMAN IN THE GRAY HOUSE)

31. LE LOCATAIRE. Paris: Nouvelle Revue Française (Gallimard), 1934. 256p.

_______. In an untitled collection with MONSIEUR LA SOURIS and LA MARIE DU PORT. Paris: Gallimard, 1953. 444p.

_______. Paris: Gallimard, 1959. 215p.

English Translations
British Editions

THE LODGER. In ESCAPE IN VAIN, tr. by Stuart Gilbert. London: George Routledge & Sons; Toronto: Musson, 1943. 280p. (Also includes ONE WAY OUT)

________. In ESCAPE IN VAIN, tr. by Stuart Gilbert. Harmondsworth: Penguin Books, 1952. 314p. (paper) (Also includes ONE WAY OUT)

American Editions

________. In ESCAPE IN VAIN, tr. by Stuart Gilbert. New York: Harcourt, Brace & Co., 1944. 282p. (Also includes ONE WAY OUT)

32. MAIGRET. Paris: Fayard, 1934. 254p.

________. Paris: Fayard, 1955. 222p. (Collection "Le Commissaire Maigret")

________. In an untitled collection with LE FOU DE BERGERAC and LA DANSEUSE DU GAI-MOULIN. Paris: Fayard, 1959. 347p. ("Bibliothèque Simenon," 8)

________. Paris: Librairie Générale Française, 1971. 190p. (Le Livre de poche, 2910)

English Translations
British Editions

MAIGRET RETURNS. In MAIGRET SITS IT OUT, tr. by Margaret Ludwig. London: George Routledge & Sons; Toronto: Musson, 1941. 275p. (Also includes THE LOCK AT CHARENTON)

________. In MAIGRET SITS IT OUT, tr. by Margaret Ludwig. Harmondsworth: Penguin Books, 1952. 254p. (paper) (Also includes THE LOCK AT CHARENTON)

American Editions

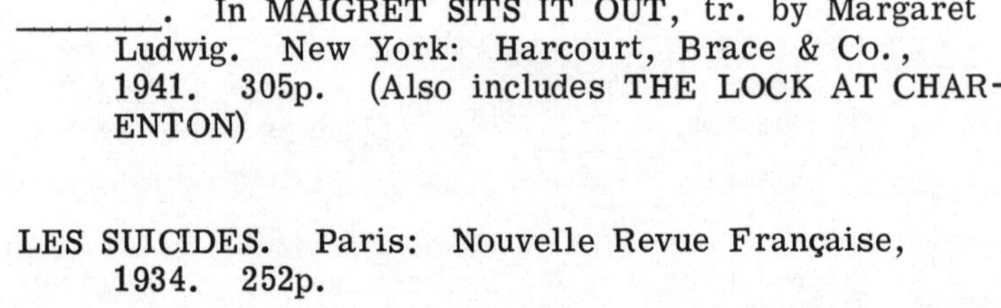

________. In MAIGRET SITS IT OUT, tr. by Margaret Ludwig. New York: Harcourt, Brace & Co., 1941. 305p. (Also includes THE LOCK AT CHARENTON)

33. LES SUICIDES. Paris: Nouvelle Revue Française, 1934. 252p.

________. Brussels: Espes, 1944. 193p.

________. Montreal: Editions Variétés, 1945. 190p.

________. In an untitled collection with LES SOEURS LACROIX and LA MAUVAISE ETOILE. Paris: Gallimard, 1953. 382p. (Edition Collective, 12)

________. Paris: Gallimard, 1958. 192p.

English Translations
British Editions

ONE WAY OUT. In ESCAPE IN VAIN, tr. by Stuart Gilbert. London: George Routledge & Sons; Toronto: Musson, 1943. 280p. (Also includes THE LODGER)

________. In ESCAPE IN VAIN, tr. by Stuart Gilbert. Harmondsworth: Penguin Books, 1952. 314p. (paper) (Also includes THE LODGER)

American Editions

In ESCAPE IN VAIN, tr. by Stuart Gilbert. New York: Harcourt, Brace & Co., 1944. 282p. (Also includes THE LODGER)

1935

34. LES CLIENTS D'AVRENOS. Paris: Nouvelle Revue Française (Gallimard), 1935. 252p.

________. In an untitled collection with 45° A L'OMBRE and QUARTIER NEGRE. Paris: Gallimard, 1951. 504p.

________. Paris: Gallimard, 1966. 212p.

35. LES PITARD. Paris: Nouvelle Revue Française, 1935. 251p.

________. Appearing in series before publication in Annales Politiques et Littéraires 104 (October 15-December 10, 1934): pp. 47-59, 103-115, 163-175, 220-231, 278-289.

________. Brussels: Espes, 1944. 192p.

________. Illustrated by Robert Noël. Paris: Grund, 1945. 163p. (some copies on finer paper). (Collection "Mazarine," 8)

________. Paris: Gallimard, 1965. 209p.

English Translations
British Editions

A WIFE AT SEA, bound with THE MURDERER and tr. by Geoffrey Sainsbury. London: Routledge & Kegan Paul, 1949. 248p.

36. QUARTIER NEGRE. Paris: Nouvelle Revue Française, 1935. 251p.

________. In an untitled collection with 45° A L'OMBRE and LES CLIENTS D'AVRENOS. Paris: Gallimand, 1951. 504p.

________. Paris: Gallimard, 1966. 207p.

1936

37. LES DEMOISELLES DE CONCARNEAU. Paris: Nouvelle Revue Française (Gallimard), 1936. 250p. (also 20 copies on "alfa" paper)

________. In an untitled collection with LA VEUVE COUDERC, LE COUP DE VAGUE and LE FILS CARDINAUD. Paris: Gallimard, 1950. 669p. (reissued in 1952)

_______. Paris: Gallimard, 1958. 188p.

English Translations
British Editions

THE BRETON SISTERS. In HAVOC BY ACCIDENT, tr. by Stuart G. Gilbert. London: George Routledge & Sons, 1943. 271p. (Also includes TALATA)

American Editions

_______. In HAVOC BY ACCIDENT, tr. by Stuart Gilbert. New York: Harcourt, Brace & Co., 1943. 312p. (Also includes TALATA)

38. L'EVADE. Paris: Nouvelle Revue Française, 1936. 250p. (Also 40 copies on "La fuma" paper)

_______, bound with LONG COURS. Paris: Gallimard, 1951. 505p.

_______. Paris: Gallimard, 1962. (Collection "Blanche")

English Translations
British Editions

THE DISINTEGRATION OF J.P.G., tr. by Geoffrey Sainsbury. London: George Routledge & Sons, Toronto: Musson, 1937. 252p.

39. LONG COURS. Paris: Nouvelle Revue Française, 1936. 284p. (Also 20 copies on "alfa" paper)

_______ bound with L'EVADE. Paris: Gallimard, 1951. 505p.

_______. Paris: Gallimard, 1966. 236p.

40. 45° A L'OMBRE. Paris: Nouvelle Revue Française, 1936. 255p. (also 20 copies on "alfa" paper)

_______. In an untitled collection with QUARTIER NEGRE and LES CLIENTS D'AVRENOS. Paris:

Gallimard, 1951. 504p.

________. Paris: Gallimard, 1967. 208p.

1937

41. L'ASSASSIN. Paris: Nouvelle Revue Française, 1937. 224p. (also 20 copies on "alfa" paper)

________. In an untitled collection with MALEMPIN and LE VOYAGEUR DE LA TOUSSAINT. Paris: Gallimard, 1951. 544p.

________. Paris: Gallimard, 1960. 224p. (Collection "Blanche")

English Translations
British Editions

THE MURDERER, bound with A WIFE AT SEA and tr. by Geoffrey Sainsbury. London: Routledge & Kegan Paul, 1947. 248p.

________, tr. by Geoffrey Sainsbury. Harmondsworth: Penguin Books, 1958. 127p. (paper)

42. LE BLANC A LUNETTES. Paris: Nouvelle Revue Française, 1937. 251p. (also 20 copies on "alfa" paper)

________. Appearing in series before publication in Annales Politiques et Littéraires 108 (October 25-December 25, 1936): pp. 425-437, 479-491, 534-547, 592-603, 646-655.

________. In an untitled collection with LA MAISON DES SEPT JEUNES FILLES and ONCLE CHARLES S'EST ENFERME. Paris: Gallimard, 1951. 406p.

________. Paris: Gallimard, 1969. 205p.

English Translations
British Editions

TALATA. In HAVOC BY ACCIDENT, tr. by Stuart Gilbert. London: George Routledge & Sons, 1943. 271p. (Also includes THE BRETON SISTERS)

________. In HAVOC BY ACCIDENT; tr. by Stuart Gilbert. Harmondsworth: Penguin Books, 1952. 284p. (paper) (Also includes THE BRETON SISTERS)

American Editions

________. In HAVOC BY ACCIDENT, tr. by Stuart Gilbert. New York: Harcourt, Brace & Co., 1943. 312p. (Also includes THE BRETON SISTERS)

43. FAUBOURG. Paris: Nouvelle Revue Française, 1937. 221p. (also 20 copies on "La fuma" paper)

________. In an untitled collection with CHEZ KRULL and LE SUSPECT. Paris: Gallimard, 1951. 480p.

________. Paris: Gallimard, 1968. 198p.

English Translations
British Editions

HOME TOWN. In ON THE DANGER LINE, tr. by Stuart Gilbert. London: George Routledge & Sons, 1944. 255p. (Also includes THE GREEN THERMOS)

________. In ON THE DANGER LINE, tr. by Stuart Gilbert. Harmondsworth: Penguin Books, 1952. 254p. (paper) (Also includes THE GREEN THERMOS)

American Editions

________. In ON THE DANGER LINE, tr. by Stuart Gilbert. New York: Harcourt, Brace & Co., 1944. 269p. (Also includes THE GREEN THERMOS)

44. LE TESTAMENT DONADIEU. Paris: Nouvelle Revue Française, 1937. 318p. (also 20 copies on "alpha" paper)

_______. Montreal: Editions Variétés, 1945. 318p.

_______ bound with LE CHALE DE MARIE DUDON. Paris: Gallimard, 1954. 450p. (Collection "Sous couverture verte," 14)

_______. Paris: Gallimard, 1960. 352p. (Collection "Blanche")

English Translations
British Editions

THE SHADOW FALLS, tr. by Stuart Gilbert. London: George Routledge & Sons; Toronto: Musson, 1945. 382p.

American Editions

_______, tr. by Stuart Gilbert. New York: Harcourt, Brace & Co., 1945. 371p.

1938

45. CEUX DE LA SOIF. Paris: Nouvelle Revue Française, 1938. 215p. (also 20 copies on "alfa" paper)

_______. In an untitled collection with LE CHEVAL BLANC and LES INCONNUS DANS LA MAISON. Paris: Gallimard, 1951. 481p.

_______. Paris: Gallimard, 1961. 227p.

46. CHEMIN SANS ISSUE. Paris: Nouvelle Revue Française, 1938. 223p. (also 20 copies on "alfa" paper)

_______. Montreal: Editions Variétés, 1945. 222p.

_______. In an untitled collection with TOURISTE DE BANANES and LES RESCAPES DU TELEMAQUE. Paris: Gallimard, 1952. 517p.

_______. Paris: Gallimard, 1959. 210p.

English Translations
British Editions

BLIND PATH. In LOST MOORINGS, tr. by Stuart Gilbert. London: George Routledge & Sons, 1946. 304p. (Also includes BANANA TOURIST)

________. In LOST MOORINGS, tr. by Stuart Gilbert. Harmondsworth: Penguin Books, 1952. 280p. (paper) (Also includes BANANA TOURIST)

American Editions

BLIND ALLEY, tr. by Stuart Gilbert. New York: Reynal & Hitchcock, 1946. 207p.

47. LE CHEVAL BLANC. Paris: Nouvelle Revue Française, 1938. 222p. (also 20 copies on "alfa" paper)

________. In an untitled collection with CEUX DE LA SOIF and LES INCONNUS DANS LA MAISON. Paris: Gallimard, 1951. 481p.

________. Paris: Gallimard, 1961. 215p. (Collection "Blanche")

48. L'HOMME QUI REGARDAIT PASSER LES TRAINS. Paris: Nouvelle Revue Française, 1938. 253p. (also 20 copies on "alfa" paper)

________. Paris: Gallimard, 1943. 247p.

________. Montreal: Editions Variétés, 1945. 253p.

________. Paris: Gallimard, 1953. 243p.

________. Paris: Gallimard, 1967. 256p.

English Translations
British Editions

THE MAN WHO WATCHED THE TRAINS GO BY, tr. by Stuart Gilbert; Toronto: Musson, 1942. 199p.

________, tr. by Stuart Gilbert. London: Pan Books,

1945. 195p.

________, tr. by Stuart Gilbert. Harmondsworth, Baltimore: Penguin Books, 1964. 183p. (paper)

American Editions

________, tr. by Stuart Gilbert. New York: Reynal & Hitchcock, 1946. 195p.

________, tr. by Stuart Gilbert. New York: Berkeley Publishing Corp., 1958. 175p. (paper)

49. LA MARIE DU PORT. Paris: Nouvelle Revue Française, 1938. 219p. (also 20 copies on "alfa" paper)

________. Montreal: Editions Variétés, 1945. 219p.

________. Prague: Editions Orbis, 1945. 113p.

________. In an untitled collection with MONSIEUR LA SOURIS and LE LOCATAIRE. Paris: Gallimard, 1953. 444p.

________. Paris: Gallimard, 1954. 255p. (Collection "Pourpre")

________. Paris: Gallimard, 1958. 197p. (Collection "Blanche")

________. Paris: Gallimard, 1959. 198p.

English Translations
British Editions

A CHIT OF A GIRL, bound with JUSTICE and tr. by Geoffrey Sainsbury. London: Routledge & Kegan Paul, 1949. 265p.

________, bound with JUSTICE and tr. by Geoffrey Sainsbury. London: Routledge & Kegan Paul, 1951. 265p. (cheaper edition)

THE GIRL IN WAITING, bound with JUSTICE, and tr. by Geoffrey Sainsbury. London: Pan Books, 1957. 253p.

50. LA MAUVAISE ETOILE. Paris: Nouvelle Revue Française, 1938. 188p. (also 20 copies on "alfa" paper)

_______. In an untitled collection with LES SOEURS LACROIX and LES SUICIDES. Paris: Gallimard, 1953. 382p.

_______. Paris: Gallimard, 1959. 149p.

51. MONSIEUR LA SOURIS. Paris: Nouvelle Revue Française, 1938. 221p.

_______. Montreal: Editions Variêtés, 1945. 221p.

_______. In an untitled collection with LE LOCATAIRE and LA MARIE DU PORT. Paris: Gallimard, 1953. 444p.

_______. Paris: Gallimard, 1959. 221p.

English Translations
British Editions

MONSIEUR LA SOURIS, bound with POISONED RELATIONS and tr. by Geoffrey Sainsbury. London: Routledge & Kegan Paul, 1950. 262p.

THE MOUSE, tr. by Robert Baldick. Harmondsworth: Penguin Books, 1966. 153p. (paper)

52. LES RESCAPES DU "TELEMAQUE." Paris: Nouvelle Revue Française, 1938. 240p. (also 20 copies on "alfa" paper)

_______. Montreal: Editions Variêtés, 1945. 240p.

_______. In an untitled collection with TOURISTE DE BANANES and CHEMIN SANS ISSUE. Paris: Gallimard, 1952. 517p.

_______. Paris: Gallimard, 1959. 229p.

English Translations
British Editions

THE SURVIVORS, tr. by Stuart Gilbert, bound with BLACK RAIN, tr. by Geoffrey Sainsbury. London: Routledge & Kegan Paul, 1949. v, 264p.

________, tr. by Stuart Gilbert, bound with BLACK RAIN, tr. by Geoffrey Sainsbury. London: Routledge & Kegan Paul, 1951. 264p. (cheaper edition)

________, tr. by Stuart Gilbert, bound with BLACK RAIN, tr. by Geoffrey Sainsbury. Harmondsworth: Penguin Books, 1965. 300p. (paper)

53. LES SEPT MINUTES (OR G7). Paris: Nouvelle Revue Française, 1938. 219p. (also 20 copies on "alfa" paper). (short stories). (Contents: LE GRAND LANGOUSTIER; LA NUIT DES SEPT MINUTES; L'ENIGME DE LA "MARIE GALANTE.") (Collection "La Renaissance de la Nouvelle")

________. Montreal: Editions Variétés, 1945. 219p.

________. In an untitled collection with LES NOCES DE POITIERS and LE RAPPORT DU GENDARME. Paris: Gallimard, 1951. 420p. (Edition Collective, 10)

________. Paris: Gallimard, 1966. 208p.

54. LES SOEURS LACROIX. Paris: Nouvelle Revue Française, 1938. 222p. (also 20 copies on "alfa" paper)

________. Montreal: Editions Variétés, 1945. 222p.

________. In an untitled collection with LA MAUVAISE ETOILE and LES SUICIDES. Paris: Gallimard, 1953. 382p.

________. Paris: Gallimard, 1958. 223p.

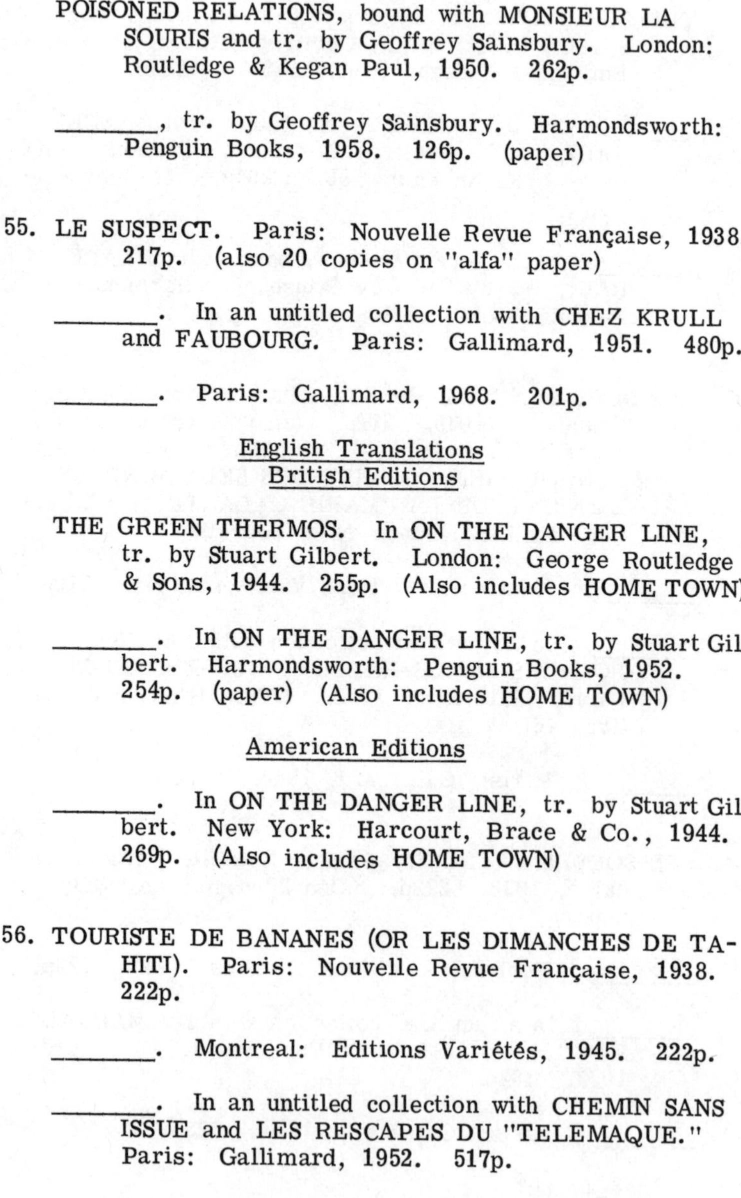

English Translations
British Editions

POISONED RELATIONS, bound with MONSIEUR LA SOURIS and tr. by Geoffrey Sainsbury. London: Routledge & Kegan Paul, 1950. 262p.

________, tr. by Geoffrey Sainsbury. Harmondsworth: Penguin Books, 1958. 126p. (paper)

55. LE SUSPECT. Paris: Nouvelle Revue Française, 1938. 217p. (also 20 copies on "alfa" paper)

________. In an untitled collection with CHEZ KRULL and FAUBOURG. Paris: Gallimard, 1951. 480p.

________. Paris: Gallimard, 1968. 201p.

English Translations
British Editions

THE GREEN THERMOS. In ON THE DANGER LINE, tr. by Stuart Gilbert. London: George Routledge & Sons, 1944. 255p. (Also includes HOME TOWN)

________. In ON THE DANGER LINE, tr. by Stuart Gilbert. Harmondsworth: Penguin Books, 1952. 254p. (paper) (Also includes HOME TOWN)

American Editions

________. In ON THE DANGER LINE, tr. by Stuart Gilbert. New York: Harcourt, Brace & Co., 1944. 269p. (Also includes HOME TOWN)

56. TOURISTE DE BANANES (OR LES DIMANCHES DE TAHITI). Paris: Nouvelle Revue Française, 1938. 222p.

________. Montreal: Editions Variétés, 1945. 222p.

________. In an untitled collection with CHEMIN SANS ISSUE and LES RESCAPES DU "TELEMAQUE." Paris: Gallimard, 1952. 517p.

________. Paris: Gallimard, 1959. 226p.

English Translations
British Editions

BANANA TOURIST. In LOST MOORINGS, tr. by Stuart Gilbert. London: George Routledge & Sons, 1946. 304p. (Also includes BLIND PATH)

________. In LOST MOORINGS, tr. by Stuart Gilbert. Harmondsworth: Penguin Books, 1952. 280p. (paper) (Also includes BLIND PATH)

57. LES TROIS CRIMES DE MES AMIS. Paris: Nouvelle Revue Française, 1938. 185p. (also 20 copies on "alfa" paper)

________ bound with L'AINE DES FERCHAUX. Paris: Gallimard, 1951. 470p.

________. Paris: Gallimard, 1962. (Collection "Blanche")

1939

58. LE BOURGMESTRE DE FURNES. Paris: Nouvelle Revue Française, 1939. 251p. (also 20 copies on "alfa" paper)

________. Paris: Gallimard, 1959. 240p. (Collection "Blanche")

________. Paris: Gallimard, 1968. 260p.

English Translations
British Editions

THE BOURGOMASTER OF FURNES, tr. by Geoffrey Sainsbury. London: Routledge & Kegan Paul; New York: British Book Service, 1952. 255p.

________, tr. by Geoffrey Sainsbury. London: Routledge & Kegan Paul, 1955. 255p. (cheaper edition).

59. CHEZ KRULL. Paris: Nouvelle Revue Française, 1939. 222p. (also 20 copies which constitute the original edition are on "alfa" paper)

________. In an untitled collection with LE SUSPECT and FAUBOURG. Paris: Gallimard, 1951. 480p.

________. Paris: Gallimard, 1968. 245p.

English Translations
British Editions

CHEZ KRULL, tr. by Daphne Woodward. In A SENSE OF GUILT. London: Hamish Hamilton, 1955. 320p. (Also includes THE HEART OF A MAN, tr. by Louise Varèse)

________, tr. by Daphne Woodward. In A SENSE OF GUILT. London: Hamish Hamilton, 1957. 320p. (Also includes THE HEART OF A MAN)

________, tr. by Daphne Woodward. London: Landsborough, 1958. 159p. (paper)

________, tr. by Daphne Woodward. London: New English Library, 1966. 159p. (paper)

________, tr. by Daphne Woodward. London: New English Library, 1968. 159p. (paper)

________, tr. by Daphne Woodward. In a collection entitled THE SECOND SIMENON OMNIBUS. London: Hamish Hamilton, 1974. 480p. (Also includes THE HEART OF A MAN, STRIPTEASE and THE WIDOWER)

60. LE COUP DE VAGUE. Paris: Gallimard, 1939. 213p. (20 copies which constitute the original edition are on "alfa" paper)

________. In an untitled collection with LA VEUVE COUDERC, LES DEMOISELLES DE CONCARNEAU and LE FILS CARDINAUD. Paris: Gallimard, 1950. 669p. (reissued in 1952)

________. Paris: Gallimard, 1960. 208p.

Titles First Published in the 1940s

1940

61. LES INCONNUS DANS LA MAISON. Paris: Nouvelle Revue Française, 1940. 227p.

________. In an untitled collection with CEUX DE LA SOIF and LE CHEVAL BLANC. Paris: Gallimard, 1951. 481p.

________. Paris: Gallimard, 1954. 255p. (Collection "Pourpre")

________. Paris: Gallimard, 1961. 231p.

English Translations
British Editions

STRANGERS IN THE HOUSE, tr. by Geoffrey Sainsbury. London: Routledge & Kegan Paul, 1951. viii, 200p.

________, tr. by Geoffrey Sainsbury. London: Brown & Watson, 1962. 159p. (paper)

________, tr. by Robert Baldick. Harmondsworth: Penguin Books, 1967. 173p. (paper)

American Editions

________, tr. by Geoffrey Sainsbury. New York: Doubleday, 1954. 186p.

62. MALEMPIN. Paris: Nouvelle Revue Française, 1940. 220p. (also 20 copies on "alfa" paper)

________. Montreal: Editions Variétés, 1945. 220p.

________. In an untitled collection with L'ASSASSIN and LE VOYAGEUR DE LA TOUSSAINT. Paris: Gallimard, 1951. 544p.

________. Paris: Gallimard, 1959. 192p.

1941

63. BERGELON. Paris: Nouvelle Revue Française, 1941. 237p.

________. In an untitled collection with L'OUTLAW, COURS D'ASSISES and IL PLEUT BERGERE... Paris: Gallimard, 1951. 753p.

________. Paris: Gallimard, 1966. 215p.

64. COUR D'ASSISES. Paris: Nouvelle Revue Française, 1941. 224p.

________. In an untitled collection with L'OUTLAW, BERGELON, and IL PLEUT BERGERE... Paris: Gallimard, 1951. 753p.

________. Paris: Gallimard, 1967. 211p.

English Translations
British Editions

JUSTICE, bound with A CHIT OF A GIRL, and tr. by Geoffrey Sainsbury. London: Routledge & Kegan Paul, 1949. 265p.

________, bound with A CHIT OF A GIRL and tr. by Geoffrey Sainsbury. London: Routledge & Kegan Paul, 1951. 265p. (cheaper edition)

________, bound with A GIRL IN WAITING and tr. by Geoffrey Sainsbury. London: Pan Books, 1957. 253p.

65. IL PLEUT BERGERE... Paris: Nouvelle Revue Française, 1941. 213p.

________. In an untitled collection with L'OUTLAW, COUR D'ASSISES and BERGELON. Paris: Gallimard, 1951. 753p.

________. Paris: Gallimard, 1966. 188p.

English Translations
British Editions

BLACK RAIN, tr. by Geoffrey Sainsbury, bound with THE SURVIVORS, tr. by Stuart Gilbert. London: Routledge & Kegan Paul, 1949. v, 264p.

________, tr. by Geoffrey Sainsbury, bound with THE SURVIVORS, tr. by Stuart Gilbert. London: Routledge & Kegan Paul, 1951. 264p. (cheaper edition)

________, tr. by Geoffrey Sainsbury, bound with THE SURVIVORS, tr. by Stuart Gilbert. Harmondsworth: Penguin Books, 1965. 300p. (paper)

American Editions

________, tr. by Geoffrey Sainsbury. New York: Reynal & Hitchcock, 1947. 176p.

66. LA MAISON DES SEPT JEUNES FILLES. Paris: Gallimard, 1941. 189p.

________. In an untitled collection with LE BLANC A LUNETTES and ONCLES CHARLES S'EST ENFERME. Paris: Gallimard, 1951. 406p.

________, bound with LE CHALE DE MARIE DUDON. Paris: Gallimard, 1969. 176p.

67. L'OUTLAW. Paris: Gallimard, 1941. 220p.

________. In an untitled collection with COUR D'ASSISES, IL PLEUT BERGERE and BERGELON. Paris: Gallimard, 1951. 753p.

________. Paris: Gallimard, 1967. 228p.

68. LE VOYAGEUR DE LA TOUSSAINT. Paris: Nouvelle Revue Française, 1941. 237p.

_______. In an untitled collection with L'ASSASSIN and MALEMPIN. Paris: Gallimard, 1951. 544p.

_______. Paris: Gallimard, 1954. 255p. (Collection "Pourpre")

_______. Paris: Gallimard, 1958. 286p. (Collection "Blanche")

English Translations
British Editions

STRANGE INHERITANCE, tr. by Geoffrey Sainsbury. London: Routledge & Kegan Paul, 1970. 222p.

_______, tr. by Geoffrey Sainsbury. London: Pan Books, 1958. 205p. (paper)

1942

69. LE FILS CARDINAUD. Paris: Nouvelle Revue Française, 1942. 189p.

_______. In an untitled collection with LA VEUVE COUDERC and LE COUP DE VAGUE. Paris: Gallimard, 1950. 669p.

_______. Paris: Gallimard, 1960. 192p. (Collection "Blanche")

English Translations
British Editions

YOUNG CARDINAUD, tr. by Richard Brain. In THE SACRIFICE. London: Hamish Hamilton, 1956. 254p. (Also includes MR. HIRE'S ENGAGEMENT, tr. by Daphne Woodward)

_______, tr. by Richard Brain. In THE SACRIFICE. London: Hamish Hamilton, 1958. 256p. (Also includes MR. HIRE'S ENGAGEMENT)

_______, tr. by Richard Brain. London: Landsborough, 1959. 160p. (paper)

________, tr. by Richard Brain. London: New English Library, 1966. 160p.

70. MAIGRET REVIENT. Paris: Nouvelle Revue Française, 1942. 528p. (short stories). (Contents: CECILE EST MORTE; LES CAVES DU MAJESTIC; LA MAISON DU JUGE.)

________. Paris: Gallimard, 1964. 439p.

________. Paris: Gallimard, 1974. 440p.

71. ONCLE CHARLES S'EST ENFERME. Paris: Nouvelle Revue Française, 1942. 214p.

________. In an untitled collection with LE BLANC A LUNETTES and LA MAISON DES SEPT JEUNES FILLES. Paris: Gallimard, 1951. 406p.

________. Paris: Gallimard, 1969. 211p.

72. LA VERITE SUR BEBE DONGE. Paris: Nouvelle Revue Française, 1942. 218p.

________. Paris: Gallimard, 1954. 189p.

________. Paris: Gallimard, 1965. 205p.

________. Paris: Gallimard, 1966. 216p.

English Translations
British Editions

THE TRIAL OF BEBE DONGE, tr. by Geoffrey Sainsbury. London: Routledge & Kegan Paul, 1952. 184p.

________, tr. by Geoffrey Sainsbury. London: Routledge & Kegan Paul, 1955. 184p. (cheaper edition)

American Editions

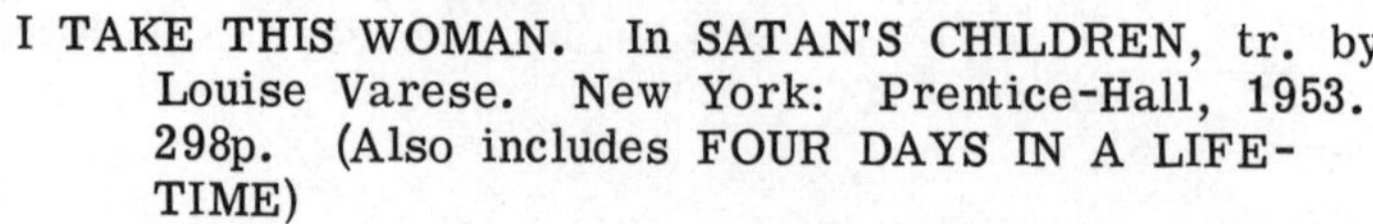

I TAKE THIS WOMAN. In SATAN'S CHILDREN, tr. by Louise Varese. New York: Prentice-Hall, 1953. 298p. (Also includes FOUR DAYS IN A LIFETIME)

73. LA VEUVE COUDERC. Paris: Nouvelle Revue Française, 1942. 236p.

________. In an untitled collection with LE COUP DE VAGUE, LES DEMOISELLES DE CONCARNEAU and LE FILS CARDINAUD. Paris: Gallimard, 1950. 669p.

________. Paris: Gallimard, 1971. 191p.

English Translations
British Editions

TICKET OF LEAVE, tr. by John Petrie. London: Routledge & Kegan Paul; New York: British Book Service, 1954. 185p.

________, tr. by John Petrie. London: Routledge & Kegan Paul, 1957. 185p. (cheaper edition)

________, tr. by John Petrie. Harmondsworth: Penguin Books, 1965. 152p. (paper)

American Editions

THE WIDOW, tr. by John Petrie, bound with MAGICIAN, tr. by Helen Sebba. New York: Doubleday, 1955. 314p.

1943

74. LES DOSSIERS DE L'AGENCE O. Paris: Nouvelle Revue Française, 1943. 666p. (short stories)

________. Paris: Gallimard, 1950. 669p.

________. Paris: Gallimard, 1964. 598p.

________. Paris: Gallimard, 1974. 610p.

75. LE PETIT DOCTEUR. Paris: Nouvelle Revue Française, 1943. 589p. (short stories)

________. Paris: Gallimard, 1949. 591p.

________. Paris: Gallimard, 1964. 529p.

________. Paris: Gallimard, 1974. 540p.

1944

76. LES NOUVELLES ENQUETES DE MAIGRET. Paris: Nouvelle Revue Française, 1944. 526p. (short stories)

________. Paris: Gallimard, 1951. 528p.

________. Paris: Gallimard, 1964. 484p. (Collection "Policier Club")

________. Paris: Gallimard, 1974. 488p.

77. LE RAPPORT DU GENDARME. Paris: Nouvelle Revue Française, 1944. 178p.

________. In an untitled collection with LES NOCES DE POITIERS and G7. Paris: Gallimard, 1951. 420p. (Edition Collective, 10)

________. Paris: Gallimard, 1959. 219p.

English Translations
British Editions

THE GENDARMES REPORT, bound with WINDOW OVER THE WAY and tr. by Geoffrey Sainsbury. London: Routledge & Kegan Paul, 1951. 291p.

78. SIGNE PICPUS. Paris: Nouvelle Revue Française, 1944. 710p. (short stories) (Also includes L' INSPECTEUR CADAVRE, FELICIE EST LA and

NOUVELLES EXOTIQUES)

________. Paris: Gallimard, 1950. 713p. (Also includes L'INSPECTEUR CADAVRE, FELICIE EST LA and NOUVELLES EXOTIQUES)

________, ed. by J. B. C. Grundy. London: George G. Harrap, 1952. 169p.

________. Paris: Gallimard, 1964. 601p. (Also includes L'INSPECTEUR CADAVRE, FELICIE EST LA and NOUVELLES EXOTIQUES)

________. Paris: Gallimard, 1974. 610p. (Same contents as previous entry.)

English Translations
British Editions

TO ANY LENGTHS, bound with MAIGRET ON HOLIDAY and tr. by Geoffrey Sainsbury. vi, 274p.

________, tr. by Geoffrey Sainsbury. Harmondsworth: Penguin Books. 127p. (paper)

1945

79. L'AINE DES FERCHAUX. Paris: Gallimard, 1945. 295p. (includes 20 copies on linen paper)

________. Bound with LES TROIS CRIMES DE MES AMIS. Paris: Gallimard, 1951. 470p.

________. Paris: Gallimard, 1962.

English Translations
British Editions

MAGNET OF DOOM, tr. by George Sainsbury. London: George Routledge & Sons; Toronto: Musson, 1948. v, 279p.

________, tr. by George Sainsbury. London: Routledge & Kegan Paul, 1951. 279p. (cheaper edition)

________, tr. by George Sainsbury. London: Pan

Books, 1956. 256p. (paper)

American Editions

THE FIRST BORN. (no translator). New York: Reynal & Hitchcock, 1949. 310p.

80. LA FENETRE DES ROUET. Illustrated by Chapelain de Midy. Paris: Editions de La Jeune Parque, 1945. 221p. (also 25 copies on white "vélin" paper)

________. Paris: Editions de La Jeune Parque, 1946. 219p. (also 25 copies on "vélvin" paper)

________. Paris: Presses de la Cité, 1952. 219p.

________. In an untitled collection with UN NOUVEAU DANS LA VILLE and LE PASSAGER CLANDESTIN. Paris: Presses de la Cité, 1958. 320p. (Collection "Trio," 4)

________. Paris: Presses de la Cité, 1964. 187p.

________. Paris: Presses de la Cité, 1967. 192p. (paper) (Collection "Presses-Pocket," 561)

________. Paris: Presses de la Cité, 1969. 221p. ("Nouvelle Collection brochée")

English Translations
British Editions

ACROSS THE STREET, tr. by John Petrie. London: Routledge & Kegan Paul, 1954. 183p.

________, tr. by John Petrie. London: Routledge & Kegan Paul, 1957. 183p. (cheaper edition)

81. LA FUITE DU MONSIEUR MONDE. Paris: Editions de la Jeune Parque, 1945. 211p.

________. Brussels: Editions Libres, 1945. 189p.

________. Paris: Presses de la Cité, 1952. 216p.

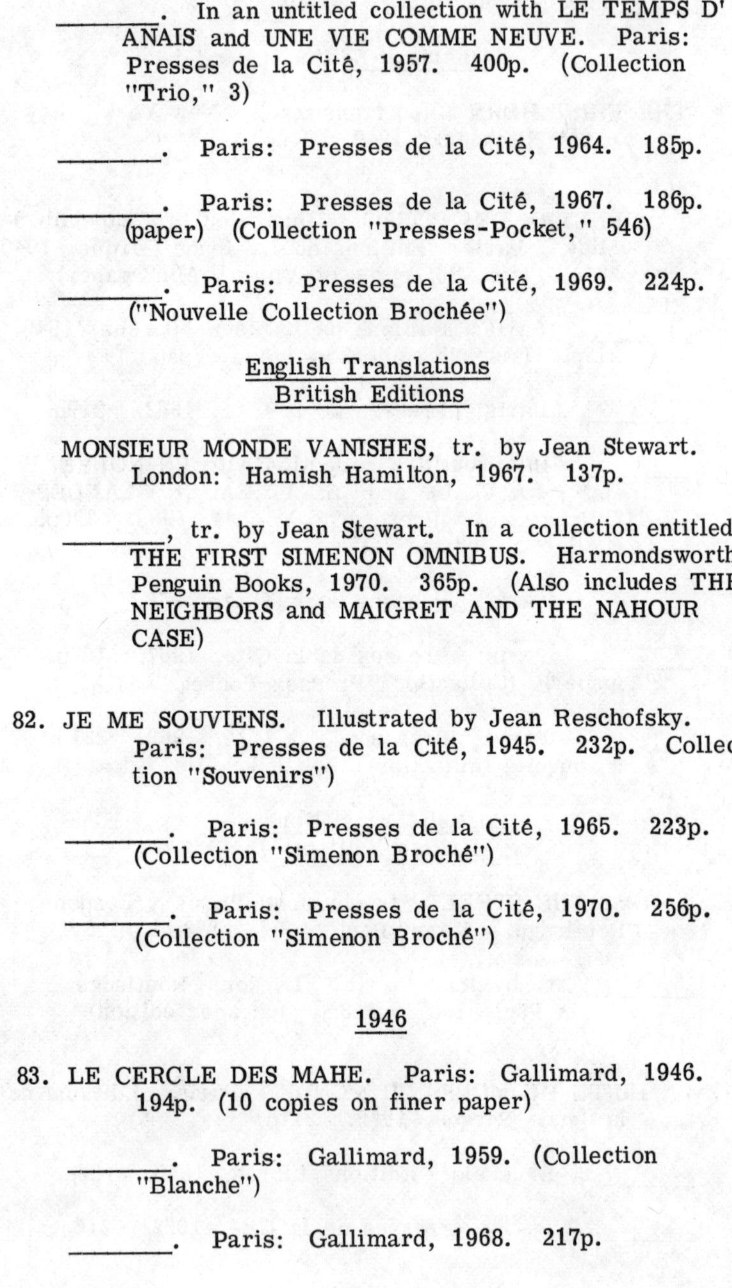

________. In an untitled collection with LE TEMPS D'ANAIS and UNE VIE COMME NEUVE. Paris: Presses de la Cité, 1957. 400p. (Collection "Trio," 3)

________. Paris: Presses de la Cité, 1964. 185p.

________. Paris: Presses de la Cité, 1967. 186p. (paper) (Collection "Presses-Pocket," 546)

________. Paris: Presses de la Cité, 1969. 224p. ("Nouvelle Collection Brochée")

English Translations
British Editions

MONSIEUR MONDE VANISHES, tr. by Jean Stewart. London: Hamish Hamilton, 1967. 137p.

________, tr. by Jean Stewart. In a collection entitled THE FIRST SIMENON OMNIBUS. Harmondsworth: Penguin Books, 1970. 365p. (Also includes THE NEIGHBORS and MAIGRET AND THE NAHOUR CASE)

82. JE ME SOUVIENS. Illustrated by Jean Reschofsky. Paris: Presses de la Cité, 1945. 232p. Collection "Souvenirs")

________. Paris: Presses de la Cité, 1965. 223p. (Collection "Simenon Broché")

________. Paris: Presses de la Cité, 1970. 256p. (Collection "Simenon Broché")

1946

83. LE CERCLE DES MAHE. Paris: Gallimard, 1946. 194p. (10 copies on finer paper)

________. Paris: Gallimard, 1959. (Collection "Blanche")

________. Paris: Gallimard, 1968. 217p.

84. LES NOCES DE POITIERS. Paris: Gallimard, 1946. 179p. (10 copies on finer paper)

________. In an untitled collection with LE RAPPORT DU GENDARME and G7. Paris: Gallimard, 1951. 420p. ("Edition Collective," 10)

________. Paris: Gallimard, 1960. 192p. (Collection "Blanche")

85. TROIS CHAMBRES A MANHATTAN. Paris: Presses de la Cité, 1946. 248p.

________. Paris: Fayard, 1954. (Collection "Le Livre de demain")

________. In an untitled collection with LETTRE A MON JUGE and TANTE JEANNE. Paris: Presses de la Cité, 1956. 416p. (Collection "Trio," 2)

________. Paris: Presses de la Cité, 1960. 251p.

________. Paris: Presses de la Cité, 1964. 215p.

________. Paris: Presses de la Cité, 1965. 191p. (paper) (Collection "Presses-Pocket," 120)

________. Paris: Presses de la Cité, 1969. 224p. ("Nouvelle Collection Brochée")

English Translations
British Editions

THREE BEDS IN MANHATTAN, tr. by Lawrence G. Blochman. Garden City, N.Y.: Doubleday, 1964. 190p.

1947

86. AU BOUT DU ROULEAU. Paris: Presses de la Cité, 1947. 246p. (There are 250 numbered copies on "alfa" paper.)

________. In an untitled collection with LA NEIGE ETAIT SALE and LE DESTIN DES MALOU.

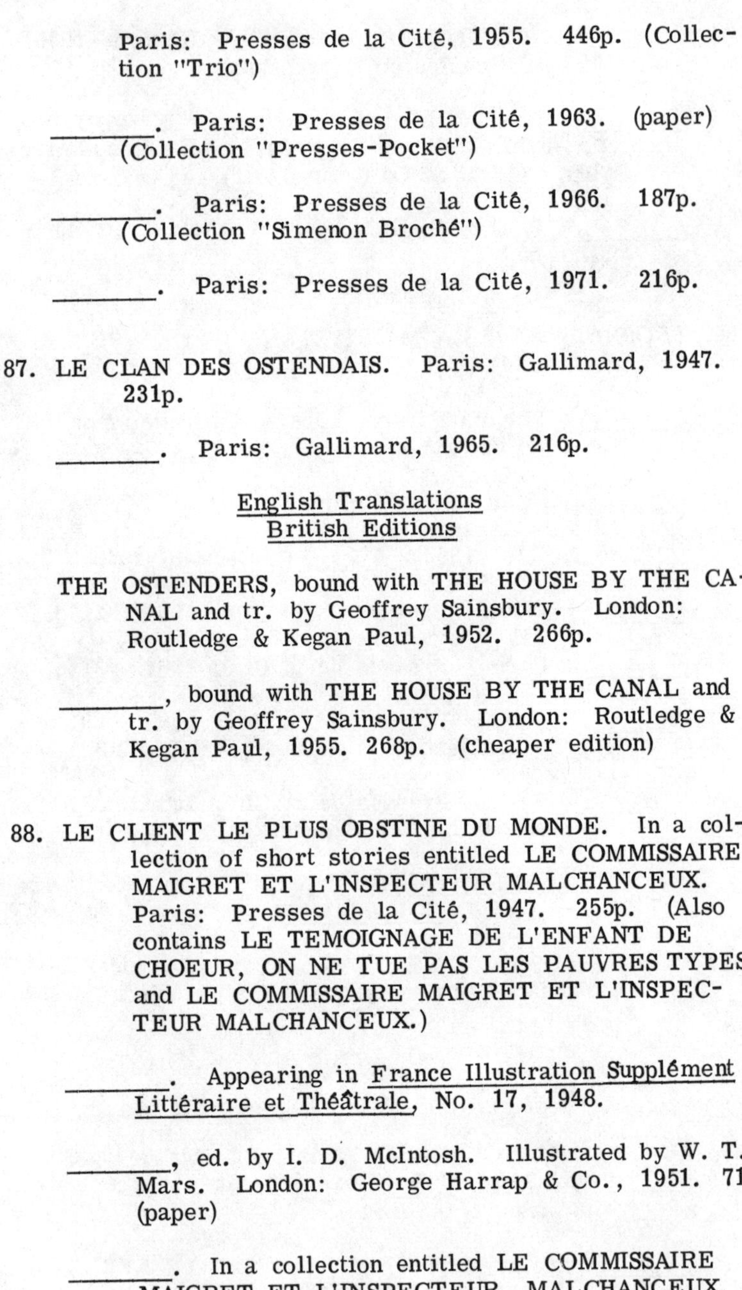

Paris: Presses de la Cité, 1955. 446p. (Collection "Trio")

________. Paris: Presses de la Cité, 1963. (paper) (Collection "Presses-Pocket")

________. Paris: Presses de la Cité, 1966. 187p. (Collection "Simenon Broché")

________. Paris: Presses de la Cité, 1971. 216p.

87. LE CLAN DES OSTENDAIS. Paris: Gallimard, 1947. 231p.

________. Paris: Gallimard, 1965. 216p.

<u>English Translations</u>
<u>British Editions</u>

THE OSTENDERS, bound with THE HOUSE BY THE CANAL and tr. by Geoffrey Sainsbury. London: Routledge & Kegan Paul, 1952. 266p.

________, bound with THE HOUSE BY THE CANAL and tr. by Geoffrey Sainsbury. London: Routledge & Kegan Paul, 1955. 268p. (cheaper edition)

88. LE CLIENT LE PLUS OBSTINE DU MONDE. In a collection of short stories entitled LE COMMISSAIRE MAIGRET ET L'INSPECTEUR MALCHANCEUX. Paris: Presses de la Cité, 1947. 255p. (Also contains LE TEMOIGNAGE DE L'ENFANT DE CHOEUR, ON NE TUE PAS LES PAUVRES TYPES and LE COMMISSAIRE MAIGRET ET L'INSPECTEUR MALCHANCEUX.)

________. Appearing in <u>France Illustration Supplément Littéraire et Théâtrale</u>, No. 17, 1948.

________, ed. by I. D. McIntosh. Illustrated by W. T. Mars. London: George Harrap & Co., 1951. 71p. (paper)

________. In a collection entitled LE COMMISSAIRE MAIGRET ET L'INSPECTEUR, MALCHANCEUX.

Paris: Presses de la Cité, 1952. 223p. (Same contents as the 1947 edition)

________, edited by I. D. McIntosh. Illustrated by W. T. Mars. Boston: Heath, 1954. 71p.

English Translations
American Editions

THE MOST OBSTINATE MAN IN PARIS, tr. by L. G. Blochman. In a collection entitled THE SHORT CASES OF INSPECTOR MAIGRET. Garden City, N.Y.: Doubleday, 1959. 188p. (Also includes MAIGRET'S CHRISTMAS, JOURNEY BACKWARD INTO TIME and THE OLD LADY OF BAYEUX)

89. LE COMMISSAIRE MAIGRET ET L'INSPECTEUR MALCHANCEUX. Paris: Presses de la Cité, 1947. 255p. (short stories). (Also contains LE TEMOIGNAGE DE L'ENFANT DE CHOEUR, LE CLIENT LE PLUS OBSTINE DU MONDE and ON NE TUE PAS LES PAUVRES TYPES.)

________. Paris: Presses de la Cité, 1952. 223p. (Same contents as first edition)

90. LETTRE A MON JUGE. Paris: Presses de la Cité, 1947. 255p.

________. Paris: Presses de la Cité, 1952. 224p.

________. In an untitled collection with TROIS CHAMBRES A MANHATTAN and TANTE JEANNE. Paris: Presses de la Cité, 1956. 416p. (Collection "Trio," 2)

________. Paris: Presses de la Cité, 1964. 223p.

________. Paris: Presses de la Cité, 1965. 192p. (paper) (Collection "Presses-Pocket," 233)

________. Paris: Presses de la Cité, 1967. 256p. (Collection "Romans")

________. Paris: Presses de la Cite, 1971. 252p.

English Translations
British Editions

ACT OF PASSION, tr. by Louise Varèse. London: Routledge & Kegan Paul, 1953. 224p.

________, tr. by Louise Varèse. London: Routledge & Kegan Paul, 1956. 236p. (cheaper edition)

________, tr. by Louise Varèse. Harmondsworth: Penguin Books, 1965. 216p. (paper)

American Editions

________, tr. by Louise Varèse. New York: Prentice-Hall, 1952. 239p.

91. MAIGRET A NEW YORK. Paris: Presses de la Cité, 1947. 253p.

________. Paris: Presses de la Cité, 1950.

________. Paris: Presses de la Cité, 1952. 217p.

________. Paris: Presses de la Cité, 1973. 190p. (paper) (Collection "Presses-Pocket," 988)

English Translations
British Editions

MAIGRET IN NEW YORK'S UNDERWORLD, tr. by Adrienne Foulke. Garden City, N.Y.: Doubleday, 1955. 190p. (Published for the Crime Club)

MAIGRET IN NEW YORK, tr. by Adrienne Foulke and bound with IN SO MANY STEPS TO DEATH by Agatha Christie, and DEATH IN LILAC TIME by Frances Crane. New York: Detective Book Club, 1955. 455p.

INSPECTOR MAIGRET IN NEW YORK'S UNDERWORLD, tr. by Adrienne Foulke. New York: New American Library, 1956. 127p. (paper)

________, tr. by Adrienne Foulke. New York: New American Library, 1964. 128p. (paper)

92. MAIGRET SE FACHE. Paris: Presses de la Cité, 1947. 253p.

________, bound with LA PIPE DE MAIGRET. Paris: Presses de la Cité, 1950. 217p.

________, bound with LA PIPE DE MAIGRET. Paris: Presses de la Cité, 1962. 190p.

________, bound with LA PIPE DE MAIGRET. Paris: Presses de la Cité, 1969. 256p.

________, bound with LA PIPE DE MAIGRET. Paris: Presses de la Cité, 1970. 190p. (paper) (Collection "Presses-Pocket," 794)

93. ON NE TUE PAS LES PAUVRES TYPES. In a collection of short stories entitled LE COMMISSAIRE MAIGRET ET L'INSPECTEUR MALCHANCEUX. Paris: Presses de la Cité, 1947. 255p. (Also contains LE TEMOIGNAGE DE L'ENFANT DE CHOEUR, LE CLIENT LE PLUS OBSTINE DU MONDE, and LE COMMISSAIRE MAIGRET ET L'INSPECTEUR MALCHANCEUX)

________. Appearing in Les Oeuvres Libres, No. 19, 1947.

________. In a collection entitled LE COMMISSAIRE MAIGRET ET L"INSPECTEUR MALCHANCEUX. Paris: Presses de la Cité, 1952. 223p. (Same contents as 1947 edition)

________, edited by Geoffrey Goodall. Illustrated by Desmond Knight. London: Macmillan; New York: St. Martin's Press, 1966. 71p.

94. LE PASSAGER CLANDESTIN. Paris: Editions de la Jeune Parque, 1947. 219p.

________. Paris: Presses de la Cité, 1952. 219p.

________. In an untitled collection with UN NOUVEAU DANS LA VILLE and LA FENETRE DES ROUET. Paris: Presses de la Cité, 1958. 320p. (Collection "Trio," 4)

________. Paris: Presses de la Cité, 1966. 189p. (Collection "Simenon broché")

________. Paris: Presses de la Cité, 1970. 212p. (Collection "Simenon broché")

English Translations
British Editions

THE STOWAWAY, tr. by Nigel Ryan. London: Hamish Hamilton, 1957. 186p.

________, tr. by Nigel Ryan. London: World Distributors, 1960. 159p. (paper)

95. LA PIPE DE MAIGRET. Paris: Presses de la Cité, 1947. Presses de la Cité, 1947.

________, bound with MAIGRET SE FACHE. Paris: Presses de la Cité, 1950. 217p.

________, edited by Cornelissen Altman. Amsterdam: Meulenhoff, 1958. 57p. (A 31-page vocabulary included)

________, bound with MAIGRET SE FACHE. Paris: Presses de la Cité, 1962. 190p.

________. Stuttgart: Klett, 1963. 56p.

________. The Hague: Van Goor Zonen, 1964. 30p.

________, ed. by Geoffrey Goodall. London: Macmillan; New York: St. Martin's Press, 1965. 72p. (reprinted in 1966, 1970, 1971)

________. In a collection entitled TROIS NOUVELLES, edited by Frank W. Lindsay and Anthony Nazarro. Illustrated by Allyn Amundson. New York: Appleton-Century-Crofts, 1966. vi, 228p. (paper) (Also includes MAIGRET ET L'INSPECTEUR MALGRACIEUX and SOUS PEINE DE MORT)

________, bound with MAIGRET SE FACHE. Paris:

Presses de la Cité, 1969. 256p.

________, bound with MAIGRET SE FACHE. Paris: Presses de la Cité, 1970. 190p. (paper) (Collection "Presses-Pocket," 794)

96. LE TEMOIGNAGE DE L'ENFANT DE CHOEUR. In a collection of short stories entitled LE COMMISSAIRE MAIGRET ET L'INSPECTEUR MALCHANCEUX. Paris: Presses de la Cité, 1947. 255p.

________. Illustrated by W. T. Mars. London: George Harrap & Co., 1949. 64p. (paper)

________. Bound with LE VIEILLARD AU PORTE-MINE. Edited by H. J. Lijfering. Amsterdam: Meulenhoff; 1951. 112p. (Collection "Les Meilleurs Auteurs Français," 116)

________, edited by Ake Bergh. Illustrated by W. T. Mars. Stockholm: Almquist and Wiksell, 1952. 54p. (Collection "Latta Spraktexterna Franska," 3) (reissued in 1961)

________. In a collection entitled LE COMMISSAIRE MAIGRET ET L'INSPECTEUR MALCHANCEUX. Paris: Presses de la Cité, 1952. 223p.

________. In a collection entitled LES TOURNANTS DANGEREUX, edited by Otis Fellows. Illustrated by Hans Alexander. New York: Appleton-Century-Crofts, 1953. 208p. (Also contains NICOLAS, LES PETITS COCHONS SANS QUEUES and L'ESCALE DE BUENAVENTURA)

________, edited by Rita Halmer. Illustrated by Hans and Isole Kohler. Stuttgart: Klett, 1960, 56p.

________. Bound with LE VIELLARD AU PORTE-MINE. Edited by H. J. Lijfering. Amsterdam: Meulenhoff, 1966. 82p.

1948

97. LE BILAN MALETRAS. Paris: Gallimard, 1948. 243p. (10 copies on finer paper)

________. Paris: Gallimard, 1967. 235p.

98. LE DESTIN DES MALOU. Paris: Presses de la Cité, 1948. 206p.

________. In an untitled collection with LA NEIGE ETAIT SALE and AU BOUT DU ROULEAU. Paris: Presses de la Cité, 1955. 446p. (Collection "Trio")

________. Paris: Presses de la Cité, 1964.

________. Paris: Presses de la Cité, 1969. 224p. ("Nouvelle Collection brochée")

________. Paris: Presses de la Cité, 1972. 187p. (Collection "Presses-Pocket," 897)

English Translations
British Editions

THE FATE OF THE MALOUS, tr. by Denis George. London: Hamish Hamilton, 1962. 160p.

________, tr. by Denis George. Harmondsworth: Penguin Books, 1966. 172p. (paper)

99. LA JUMENT PERDUE. Paris: Presses de la Cité, 1948. 221p.

________. Paris: Presses de la Cité, 1954. 223p.

________. In an untitled collection with LES FRERES RICO and LE FOND DE LA BOUTEILLE. Paris: Presses de la Cité, 1960. 404p. (Collection "Trio," 7)

________. Paris: Presses de la Cité, 1964.

________. Paris: Presses de la Cité, 1966. 192p. (Collection "Presses-Pocket," 411)

________. Paris: Presses de la Cité, 1969. 224p. ("Nouvelle Collection brochée")

100. MAIGRET ET SON MORT. Paris: Presses de la Cité, 1948.

________. Paris: Presses de la Cité, 1963. 189p.

________. Paris: Presses de la Cité, 1971. 186p. (Collection "Commissaire Maigret," 12)

________. Paris: Presses de la Cité, 1974. 192p. (Collection "Presses-Pocket," 1098)

English Translations
British Editions

MAIGRET'S SPECIAL MURDER, tr. by Jean Stewart. London: Hamish Hamilton, 1964. 188p.

________, tr. by Jean Stewart. Harmondsworth: Penguin Books, 1966. 175p. (paper)

________, tr. by Jean Stewart. In a collection entitled A MAIGRET QUARTET. London: Hamish Hamilton, 1972. 416p. (Also includes MAIGRET'S FAILURE, MAIGRET IN SOCIETY and MAIGRET AND THE LAZY BURGLARS)

American Editions

MAIGRET'S DEAD MAN, tr. by Jean Stewart. Garden City, N.Y.: Doubleday, 1964. 192p. (Published for the Crime Club)

________, tr. by Jean Stewart. In an untitled collection with ONLY THE RICH DIE YOUNG, by Hugh Pentecost and THE YELLOW VILLA, by Suzanne Blanc. Roslyn, N.Y.: Black, 1964. 467p.

101. LA NEIGE ETAIT SALE. Paris: Presses de la Cité, 1948. 246p. (also 200 copies "de luxe")

________. Dramatic adaptation by Simenon and Frédéric Dord. Appearing in Les Oeuvres Libres, Nouvelle Série, No. 57, 1951, pp. 235-302. (Also appearing in France Illustration Supplément Théâtral et Littéraire, No. 76, 1951)

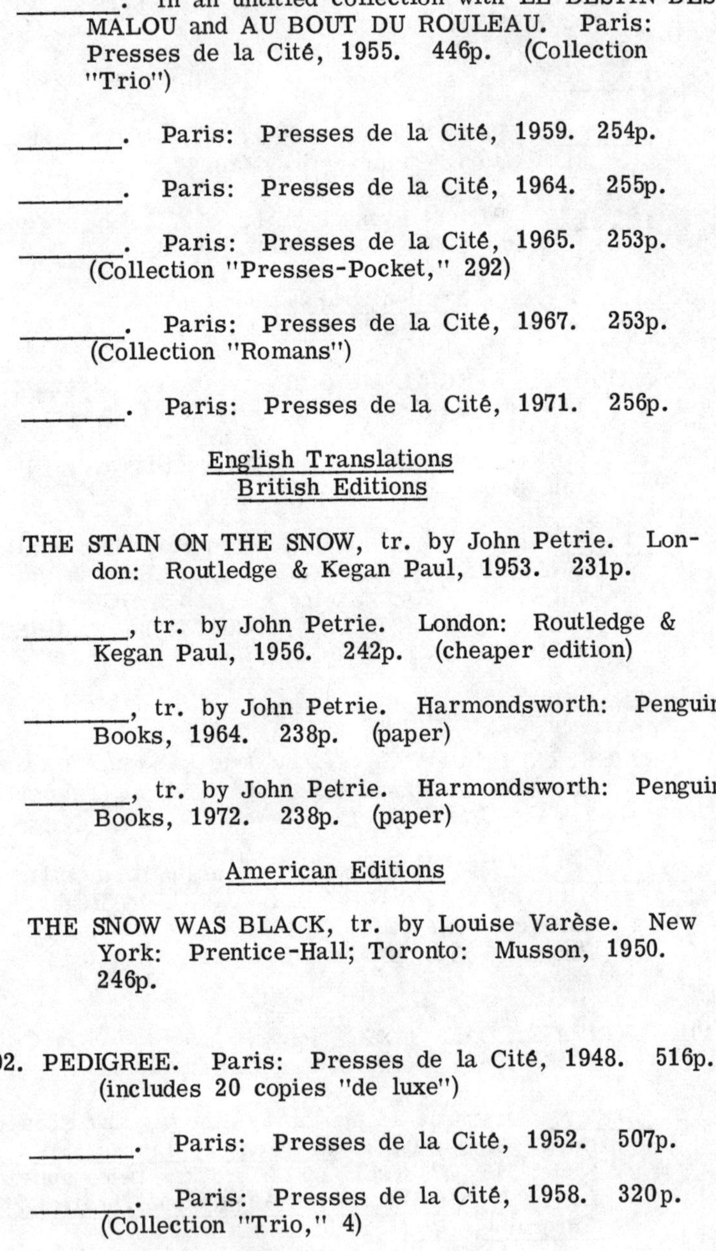

________. In an untitled collection with LE DESTIN DES MALOU and AU BOUT DU ROULEAU. Paris: Presses de la Cité, 1955. 446p. (Collection "Trio")

________. Paris: Presses de la Cité, 1959. 254p.

________. Paris: Presses de la Cité, 1964. 255p.

________. Paris: Presses de la Cité, 1965. 253p. (Collection "Presses-Pocket," 292)

________. Paris: Presses de la Cité, 1967. 253p. (Collection "Romans")

________. Paris: Presses de la Cité, 1971. 256p.

English Translations
British Editions

THE STAIN ON THE SNOW, tr. by John Petrie. London: Routledge & Kegan Paul, 1953. 231p.

________, tr. by John Petrie. London: Routledge & Kegan Paul, 1956. 242p. (cheaper edition)

________, tr. by John Petrie. Harmondsworth: Penguin Books, 1964. 238p. (paper)

________, tr. by John Petrie. Harmondsworth: Penguin Books, 1972. 238p. (paper)

American Editions

THE SNOW WAS BLACK, tr. by Louise Varèse. New York: Prentice-Hall; Toronto: Musson, 1950. 246p.

102. PEDIGREE. Paris: Presses de la Cité, 1948. 516p. (includes 20 copies "de luxe")

________. Paris: Presses de la Cité, 1952. 507p.

________. Paris: Presses de la Cité, 1958. 320p. (Collection "Trio," 4)

_______. Paris: Presses de la Cité, 1967. 3 vols. 608p. (Volume I, A L'OMBRE DE SAINT NICOLAS. 192p.; Volume II, LA MAISON ENVAHIE. 192p.; Volume III, QUAND LES LAMPES SONT ETEINTES. 224p.)

_______. Paris: Presses de la Cité, 1972. 573p. (Volume I, A L'OMBRE DE SAINT NICOLAS. 189p.; Volume II, LA MAISON ENVAHIE. 192p.; Volume III, QUAND LES LAMPES SONT ETEINTES. 192p.)

English Translations
British Editions

PEDIGREE, tr. by Robert Baldick. London: Hamish Hamilton, 1962. 543p.

_______, tr. by Robert Baldick. Harmondsworth: Penguin Books, 1965. 555p. (paper)

103. LES VACANCES DE MAIGRET. Paris: Presses de la Cité, 1948.

_______. Paris: Presses de la Cité, 1951. 223p.

_______. Paris: Presses de la Cité, 1967. 190p.

_______. In volume II of a collection entitled LES ENQUETES DU COMMISSAIRE MAIGRET. Paris: Presses de la Cité, 1967. 472p.

English Translations
British Editions

MAIGRET ON HOLIDAY, tr. by Geoffrey Sainsbury. London: Routledge & Kegan Paul, 1950. vi, 274p.

_______, tr. by Jacqueline Baldick. Harmondsworth: Penguin Books, 1970. 157p. (paper)

American Editions

NO VACATION FOR MAIGRET, tr. by Geoffrey Sainsbury. Garden City, N.Y.: Doubleday, 1953. 191p. (Pub. for the Crime Club)

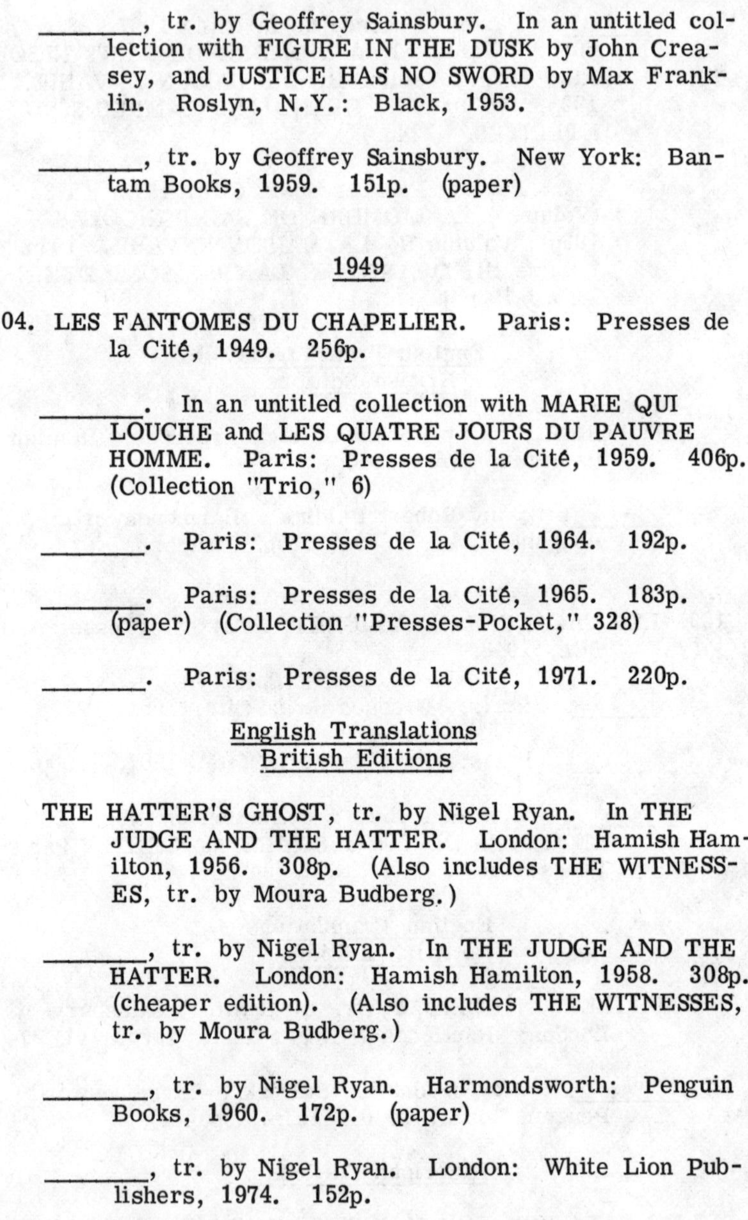

________, tr. by Geoffrey Sainsbury. In an untitled collection with FIGURE IN THE DUSK by John Creasey, and JUSTICE HAS NO SWORD by Max Franklin. Roslyn, N.Y.: Black, 1953.

________, tr. by Geoffrey Sainsbury. New York: Bantam Books, 1959. 151p. (paper)

1949

104. LES FANTOMES DU CHAPELIER. Paris: Presses de la Cité, 1949. 256p.

________. In an untitled collection with MARIE QUI LOUCHE and LES QUATRE JOURS DU PAUVRE HOMME. Paris: Presses de la Cité, 1959. 406p. (Collection "Trio," 6)

________. Paris: Presses de la Cité, 1964. 192p.

________. Paris: Presses de la Cité, 1965. 183p. (paper) (Collection "Presses-Pocket," 328)

________. Paris: Presses de la Cité, 1971. 220p.

English Translations
British Editions

THE HATTER'S GHOST, tr. by Nigel Ryan. In THE JUDGE AND THE HATTER. London: Hamish Hamilton, 1956. 308p. (Also includes THE WITNESSES, tr. by Moura Budberg.)

________, tr. by Nigel Ryan. In THE JUDGE AND THE HATTER. London: Hamish Hamilton, 1958. 308p. (cheaper edition). (Also includes THE WITNESSES, tr. by Moura Budberg.)

________, tr. by Nigel Ryan. Harmondsworth: Penguin Books, 1960. 172p. (paper)

________, tr. by Nigel Ryan. London: White Lion Publishers, 1974. 152p.

105. LE FOND DE LA BOUTEILLE. Paris: Presses de la

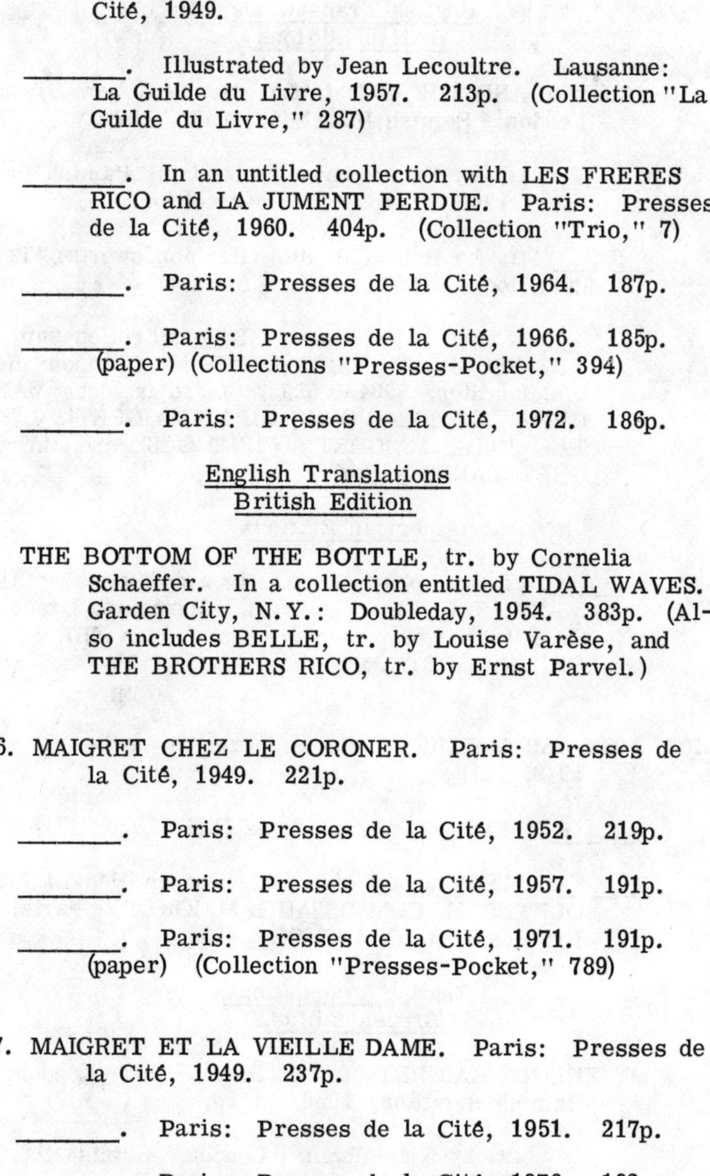

Cité, 1949.

________. Illustrated by Jean Lecoultre. Lausanne: La Guilde du Livre, 1957. 213p. (Collection "La Guilde du Livre," 287)

________. In an untitled collection with LES FRERES RICO and LA JUMENT PERDUE. Paris: Presses de la Cité, 1960. 404p. (Collection "Trio," 7)

________. Paris: Presses de la Cité, 1964. 187p.

________. Paris: Presses de la Cité, 1966. 185p. (paper) (Collections "Presses-Pocket," 394)

________. Paris: Presses de la Cité, 1972. 186p.

English Translations
British Edition

THE BOTTOM OF THE BOTTLE, tr. by Cornelia Schaeffer. In a collection entitled TIDAL WAVES. Garden City, N.Y.: Doubleday, 1954. 383p. (Also includes BELLE, tr. by Louise Varèse, and THE BROTHERS RICO, tr. by Ernst Parvel.)

106. MAIGRET CHEZ LE CORONER. Paris: Presses de la Cité, 1949. 221p.

________. Paris: Presses de la Cité, 1952. 219p.

________. Paris: Presses de la Cité, 1957. 191p.

________. Paris: Presses de la Cité, 1971. 191p. (paper) (Collection "Presses-Pocket," 789)

107. MAIGRET ET LA VIEILLE DAME. Paris: Presses de la Cité, 1949. 237p.

________. Paris: Presses de la Cité, 1951. 217p.

________. Paris: Presses de la Cité, 1970. 192p. (Collection "Presses-Pocket," 787)

English Translations
British Editions

MAIGRET AND THE OLD LADY, tr. by Robert Brain. London: Hamish Hamilton, 1958. 192p.

________, tr. by Robert Brain. London: Hamish Hamilton, 1960. 192p. (cheaper edition)

________, tr. by Robert Brain. Harmondsworth: Penguin Books, 1962. 159p. (paper)

________, tr. by Robert Brain. In a collection entitled THE SECOND MAIGRET OMNIBUS. London: Hamish Hamilton, 1964. 523p. (Also includes MAIGRET AND THE YOUNG GIRL, MAIGRET'S LITTLE JOKE, MAIGRET'S FIRST CASE and MAIGRET TAKES A ROOM.)

American Editions

________, tr. by Robert Brain. In a collection entitled MAIGRET CINQ. New York: Harcourt, Brace & Co., 1965. 523p. (Same contents as THE SECOND MAIGRET OMNIBUS.)

108. MON AMI MAIGRET. Paris: Presses de la Cité, 1949. 219p.

________. Paris: Presses de la Cité, 1956. 218p.

________. In Volume I of a collection entitled LES ENQUETES DU COMMISSAIRE MAIGRET. Paris: Presses de la Cité, 1966. 480p.

English Translations
British Editions

MY FRIEND MAIGRET, tr. by Nigel Ryan. London: Hamish Hamilton, 1956. 159p.

________, tr. by Nigel Ryan. London: Hamish Hamilton, 1958. 160p. (cheaper edition)

________, tr. by Nigel Ryan. Harmondsworth: Penguin Books, 1959. 139p. (paper)

_______, tr. by Nigel Ryan. In a collection entitled MAIGRET TRIUMPHANT. London: Hamish Hamilton, 1969. 507p. (Also includes MAIGRET AND THE BURGLAR'S WIFE, MAIGRET'S REVOLVER, MAIGRET IN COURT)

American Editions

THE METHODS OF MAIGRET, tr. by Nigel Ryan. Garden City, N.Y.: Doubleday, 1957. 192p. (Published for the Crime Club.)

_______, tr. by Nigel Ryan. New York: Bantam Books, 1959. 141p. (paper)

109. LA PREMIERE ENQUETE DE MAIGRET, 1913. Paris: Presses de la Cité, 1949. 221p.

_______. Paris: Presses de la Cité, 1953. 219p.

_______. Illustrated by Daniel Dupuy. Paris: Société Nouvelle des Editions G. P., 1965. 256p.

_______. In Volume I of a collection entitled LES ENQUETES DU COMMISSAIRE MAIGRET. Paris: Presses de la Cité, 1966. 480p.

_______. Paris: Presses de la Cité, 1971. 188p.

English Translations
British Editions

MAIGRET'S FIRST CASE, tr. by Robert Brain. London: Hamish Hamilton, 1958. 191p.

_______, tr. by Robert Brain. Harmondsworth: Penguin Books, 1961. 170p. (paper)

_______, tr. by Robert Brain. In a collection entitled THE SECOND MAIGRET OMNIBUS. London: Hamish Hamilton, 1964. 523p. (Also includes MAIGRET AND THE YOUNG GIRL, MAIGRET'S LITTLE JOKE, MAIGRET AND THE OLD LADY and MAIGRET TAKES A ROOM.)

_______, tr. by Robert Brain. London: Heinemann

Education Ltd., 1970. 191p.

American Editions

________, tr. by Robert Brain. In a collection entitled MAIGRET CINQ. New York: Harcourt, Brace & Co., 1965. 523p. (Same contents as THE SECOND MAIGRET OMNIBUS)

110. LES QUATRE JOURS DU PAUVRE HOMME. Paris: Presses de la Cité, 1949. 255p. (100 numbered copies on "vélin" paper)

________. In an untitled collection with MARIE QUI LOUCHE and LES FANTOMES DU CHAPELIER. Paris: Presses de la Cité, 1959. 406p. (Collection "Trio," 6)

________. Paris: Presses de la Cité, 1963. 247p.

________. Paris: Presses de la Cité, 1966. 187p. (Collection "Simenon broché")

________. Paris: Presses de la Cité, 1968. 243p. (paper) (Collection "Presses-Pocket," 97)

________. Paris: Presses de la Cité, 1972. 192p.

English Translations
British Editions

FOUR DAYS IN A LIFETIME, tr. by Louise Varèse. In SATAN'S CHILDREN. New York: Prentice-Hall, 1953. 298p. (Also includes I TAKE THIS WOMAN, tr. by Geoffrey Sainsbury.)

Titles First Published in the 1950s

1950

111\. L'AMIE DE MME MAIGRET. Paris: Presses de la Cité, 1950. 224p.

________. Paris: Presses de la Cité, 1952. 223p.

________. Paris: Presses de la Cité, 1967. 187p.

________. Paris: Presses de la Cité, 1974. 187p. (paper) (Collection "Presses-Pocket," 1066)

English Translations
British Editions

MADAME MAIGRET'S FRIEND, tr. by Helen Sebba. London: Hamish Hamilton, 1960. 189p.

________, tr. by Helen Sebba. Harmondsworth: Penguin Books, 1967. 159p. (paper)

________, tr. by Helen Sebba. In a collection entitled MAIGRET: A FIFTH OMNIBUS. London: Hamish Hamilton, 1973. 411p. (Also includes MAIGRET ON THE DEFENSIVE, THE PATIENCE OF MAIGRET and MAIGRET TAKES THE WATERS.)

American Editions

MADAME MAIGRET'S OWN CASE, tr. by Helen Sebba. Garden City, N.Y.: Doubleday, 1959. (Published for the Crime Club.)

________, tr. by Helen Sebba. New York: Pyramid, 1963. 160p. (paper)

112. L'ENTERREMENT DE MONSIEUR BOUVET. Paris: Presses de la Cité, 1950. 223p.

_______. In an untitled collection with LE GRAND BOB and ANTOINE ET JULIE. Paris: Presses de la Cité, 1961. 407p. (Collection "Trio," 8)

_______. Paris: Presses de la Cité, 1962. 183p. (paper) (Collection "Presses-Pocket," 84)

_______. Paris: Presses de la Cité, 1966. 192p. (Collection "Simenon broché")

_______. Paris: Presses de la Cité, 1971. 216p.

English Translations
British Editions

INQUEST ON BOUVET, tr. by Eugene MacCown. London: Hamish Hamilton, 1958. 189p.

_______, tr. by Eugene MacCown. Harmondsworth: Penguin Books, 1962. 151p. (paper)

American Editions

THE BURIAL OF MONSIEUR BOUVET, tr. by Eugene MacCown. In DESTINATIONS. Garden City, N.Y.: Doubleday, 1955. 320p. (Also includes THE HITCHHIKER, tr. by Norman Denay)

113. UN NOUVEAU DANS LA VILLE. Paris: Presses de la Cité, 1950. 220p.

_______. In an untitled collection with LA FENETRE DES ROUET and LE PASSAGER CLANDESTIN. Paris: Presses de la Cité, 1958. 320p. (Collection "Trio," 4)

_______. Paris: Presses de la Cité, 1964. 189p.

_______. Paris: Presses de la Cité, 1966. 186p. (paper) (Collection "Presses-Pocket," 454)

_______. Paris: Presses de la Cité, 1972. 188p.

114. LES PETITS COCHONS SANS QUEUES. Paris: Presses de la Cité, 1950. 224p. (Collection "Maigret")

_______. In a collection entitled TOURNANTS DANGEREUX, ed. by Otis Fellows and illustrated by Hans Alexander Mueller. New York: Appleton-Century-Crofts, 1953. 208p. (Also includes NICOLAS, LE TEMOIGNAGE DE L'ENFANT DE CHOEUR and L'ESCALE DE BUENAVENTURA)

MAIGRET ET LES PETITS COCHONS SANS QUEUES. Paris: Presses de la Cité, 1957. 222p. (Collection "Maigret")

_______. In Volume II of a collection entitled LES ENQUETES DU COMMISSAIRE MAIGRET. Paris: Presses de la Cité, 1967. 472p.

_______. Paris: Presses de la Cité, 1971. 190p.

115. TANTE JEANNE. Paris: Presses de la Cité, 1950, 220p.

_______. Paris: Presses de la Cité, 1952. 220p.

_______. In an untitled collection with TROIS CHAMBRES A MANHATTAN and LETTRE A MON JUGE. Paris: Presses de la Cité, 1956. 416p. (Collection "Trio," 2)

_______. Paris: Presses de la Cité, 1964. 189p. (Collection "Simenon")

_______. Paris: Presses de la Cité, 1966. 192p. (paper) (Collection "Presses-Pocket," 424)

_______. Paris: Presses de la Cité, 1972. 217p.

English Translations
British Editions

AUNT JEANNE, tr. by Geoffrey Sainsbury. London: Routledge & Kegan Paul, 1953. 186p.

_______, tr. by Geoffrey Sainsbury. London: Routledge & Kegan Paul, 1956. 186p. (cheaper edition)

116. LES VOLETS VERTS. Paris: Presses de la Cité, 1950. 223p.

_______. Paris: Presses de la Cité, 1965. 219p. (Collection "Simenon broché")

_______. Paris: Presses de la Cité, 1967. 250p. (Collection "Romans")

_______. Paris: Presses de la Cité, 1971. 222p.

English Translations
British Editions

THE HEART OF A MAN, tr. by Louise Varèse. In A SENSE OF GUILT. London: Hamish Hamilton, 1955. 320p. (Also includes CHEZ KRULL, tr. by Daphne Woodward.)

_______, tr. by Louise Varèse. In A SENSE OF GUILT. London: Hamish Hamilton, 1957. 320p. (cheaper edition) (Also includes CHEZ KRULL, tr. by Daphne Woodward.)

_______, tr. by Louise Varèse. London: Landsborough, 1958. 160p. (paper)

_______, tr. by Louise Varèse. London: New English Library, 1968. 154p. (paper)

_______, tr. by Louise Varèse. In a collection entitled THE SECOND SIMENON OMNIBUS. London: Hamish Hamilton, 1974. 480p. (Also includes CHEZ KRULL, STRIPTEASE and THE WIDOWER.)

American Editions

_______, tr. by Louise Varèse. New York: Prentice-Hall; Toronto: McLeod, 1951. 213p.

1951

117. MAIGRET AU "PICRATT'S." Paris: Presses de la Cité, 1951. 223p.

________. In Volume II a collection entitled LES ENQUETES DU COMMISSAIRE MAIGRET. Paris: Presses de la Cité, 1967. 472p.

________. Paris: Presses de la Cité, 1970. 192p. (paper) (Collection "Presses-Pocket," 788)

________. Kalmthout, Belgium: Beckers, 1972. 215p. (Collection "Le Panthéon du Crime")

English Translations
British Editions

MAIGRET IN MONTMARTRE, tr. by Daphne Woodward. In MAIGRET RIGHT AND WRONG. London: Hamish Hamilton, 1954. 286p. (Also includes MAIGRET'S MISTAKE, tr. by Alan Hodge.)

________, tr. by Daphne Woodward. In MAIGRET RIGHT AND WRONG. London: Hamish Hamilton, 1957. 286p. (Also includes MAIGRET'S MISTAKE, tr. by Alan Hodge.)

________, tr. by Daphne Woodward. Harmondsworth: Penguin Books, 1958. 139p. (paper)

________, tr. by Daphne Woodward. In a collection entitled A MAIGRET OMNIBUS. London: Hamish Hamilton, 1962. 525p. (Also includes MAIGRET'S MISTAKE, MAIGRET HAS SCRUPLES, MAIGRET AND THE RELUCTANT WITNESSES and MAIGRET GOES TO SCHOOL.)

________, tr. by Daphne Woodward. In MAIGRET RIGHT AND WRONG. London: Hamish Hamilton, 1967. 286p. (Also includes MAIGRET'S MISTAKE, tr. by Alan Hodges.)

American Editions

INSPECTOR MAIGRET AND THE STRANGLED STRIPPER, tr. by Cornelia Schaeffer. Garden City, N.Y.:

Doubleday, 1954. 188p. (Published for the Crime Club)

________, tr. by Cornelia Schaeffer. New York: American Library, 1964. 127p. (paper)

MAIGRET IN MONTMARTRE, tr. by Daphne Woodward. In a collection entitled FIVE TIMES MAIGRET. New York: Harcourt, Brace & Co., 1964. 525p. (Same contents as A MAIGRET OMNIBUS.)

118. MAIGRET EN MEUBLE. Paris: Presses de la Cité, 1951. 223p.

________. Paris: Presses de la Cité, 1968. 187p.

________. Paris: Presses de la Cité, 1973. 187p. (paper) (Collection "Presses-Pocket," 1038)

English Translations
British Editions

MAIGRET TAKES A ROOM, tr. by Robert Brain. London: Hamish Hamilton, 1960. 192p.

________, tr. by Robert Brain. In a collection entitled THE SECOND MAIGRET OMNIBUS. London: Hamish Hamilton, 1964. 523p. (Also includes MAIGRET AND THE YOUNG GIRL, MAIGRET'S LITTLE JOKE, MAIGRET AND THE OLD LADY and MAIGRET'S FIRST CASE.)

________, tr. by Robert Brain. Harmondsworth: Penguin Books, 1965. 154p. (paper)

American Editions

MAIGRET RENTS A ROOM, tr. by Robert Brain. Garden City, N.Y.: Doubleday, 1961. 192p.

________, tr. by Robert Brain. Roslyn, N.Y.: W. J. Black, 1961. 132p.

________, tr. by Robert Brain. New York: Popular Library, 1962. 124p. (paper)

________, tr. by Robert Brain. In a collection entitled MAIGRET CINQ. New York: Harcourt, Brace & Co., 1965. 523p. (Same contents as THE SECOND MAIGRET OMNIBUS)

119. MAIGRET ET LA GRANDE PERCHE. Paris: Presses de la Cité, 1951. 222p.

________. Paris: Presses de la Cité, 1962. 191p. (Collection "Maigret")

________. Paris: Presses de la Cité, 1970. 190p. (paper) (Collection "Presses-Pocket," 795)

English Translations
British Editions

MAIGRET AND THE BURGLAR'S WIFE, tr. by J. Maclaren-Ross. London: Hamish Hamilton, 1955. 159p.

________, tr. by J. Maclaren-Ross. London: Hamish Hamilton, 1957. 160p. (cheaper edition)

________, tr. by J. Maclaren-Ross. Harmondsworth: Penguin Book, 1959. 140p. (paper)

________, tr. by J. Maclaren-Ross. In a collection entitled MAIGRET TRIUMPHANT. London: Hamish Hamilton, 1969. 507p. (Also includes MAIGRET'S REVOLVER, MY FRIEND MAIGRET, MAIGRET IN COURT and MAIGRET AFRAID.)

American Editions

INSPECTOR MAIGRET AND THE BURGLAR'S WIFE, tr. by J. Maclaren-Ross. Garden City, N.Y.: Doubleday, 1956. 186p. (Published for the Crime Club)

________, tr. by J. Maclaren-Ross. In an untitled collection with POSTMARK MURDER by Mignon Eberhart and WANTED FOR MURDER by Nancy Routledge. Roslyn, N.Y.: W. J. Black, 1956. 472p.

120. MARIE QUI LOUCHE. Paris: Presses de la Cité,

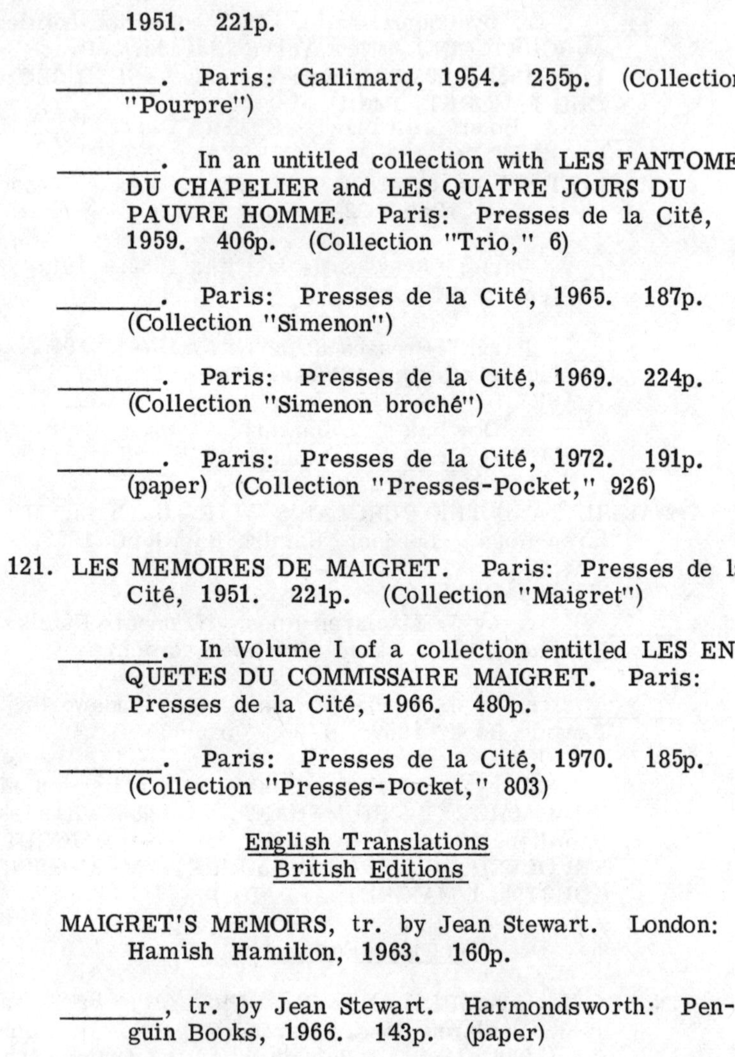

1951. 221p.

________. Paris: Gallimard, 1954. 255p. (Collection "Pourpre")

________. In an untitled collection with LES FANTOMES DU CHAPELIER and LES QUATRE JOURS DU PAUVRE HOMME. Paris: Presses de la Cité, 1959. 406p. (Collection "Trio," 6)

________. Paris: Presses de la Cité, 1965. 187p. (Collection "Simenon")

________. Paris: Presses de la Cité, 1969. 224p. (Collection "Simenon broché")

________. Paris: Presses de la Cité, 1972. 191p. (paper) (Collection "Presses-Pocket," 926)

121\. LES MEMOIRES DE MAIGRET. Paris: Presses de la Cité, 1951. 221p. (Collection "Maigret")

________. In Volume I of a collection entitled LES ENQUETES DU COMMISSAIRE MAIGRET. Paris: Presses de la Cité, 1966. 480p.

________. Paris: Presses de la Cité, 1970. 185p. (Collection "Presses-Pocket," 803)

English Translations
British Editions

MAIGRET'S MEMOIRS, tr. by Jean Stewart. London: Hamish Hamilton, 1963. 160p.

________, tr. by Jean Stewart. Harmondsworth: Penguin Books, 1966. 143p. (paper)

________. tr. by Jean Stewart. London: White Lion, 1974. 160p.

122\. UN NOEL DE MAIGRET. Bound with SEPT PETITES CROIX DANS UN CARNET and LE PETIT RESTAURANT DE TERNES. Paris: Presses de la Cité, 1951. 222p. (short stories)

_______. Bound with SEPT PETITES CROIX DANS UN CARNET and LE PETIT RESTAURANT DE TERNES. Paris: Presses de la Cité, 1963. 189p.

_______. Bound with SEPT PETITES CROIX DANS UN CARNET and LE PETIT RESTAURANT DE TERNES. Paris: Presses de la Cité, 1973. 189p. (paper) (Collection "Presses-Pocket," 1006)

English Translations
American Editions

MAIGRET'S CHRISTMAS, tr. by L. G. Blochman. In a collection of short stories entitled THE SHORT CASES OF INSPECTOR MAIGRET. Garden City, N.Y.: Doubleday, 1959. 188p. (Also includes JOURNEY BACKWARD INTO TIME, STAN THE KILLER, THE OLD LADY OF BAYEUX and THE MOST OBSTINATE MAN IN PARIS.)

123. OMNIBUS SIMENON. Paris: Gallimard, 1951. 9 vols. (A collection of Simenon's novels written before 1950)

(Volume I. LA VEUVE COUDERC, LE COUP DE VAGUE, LES DEMOISELLES DE CONCARNEAU, LE FILS CARDINAUD.
II. L'OUTLAW, COURS D'ASSISES, IL PLEUT, BERGERE..., BERGELON.
III. 45° A L'OMBRE, QUARTIER NEGRE. LES CLIENTS D'AVRENOS.
IV. LE VOYAGEUR DE LA TOUSSAINT, L'ASSASSIN, MALEMPIN.
V. LONG COURS, L'EVADE.
VI. CHEZ KRULL, LE SUSPECT, FAUBOURG
VII. LE BLANC A LUNETTES, LA MAISON DES SEPT JEUNES FILLES, ONCLE CHARLES S'EST ENFERME.
VIII. CEUX DE LA SOIF, LE CHEVAL BLANC, LES INCONNUS DANS LA MAISON.
IX. LES NOCES DE POITIERS, LE RAPPORT DU GENDARME, G7.)

_______. Volume X. Paris: Gallimard, 1952. 520p. (Volume X. TOURISTE DE BANANES, CHEMIN SANS ISSUE, LES RESCAPES DU TELEMAQUE)

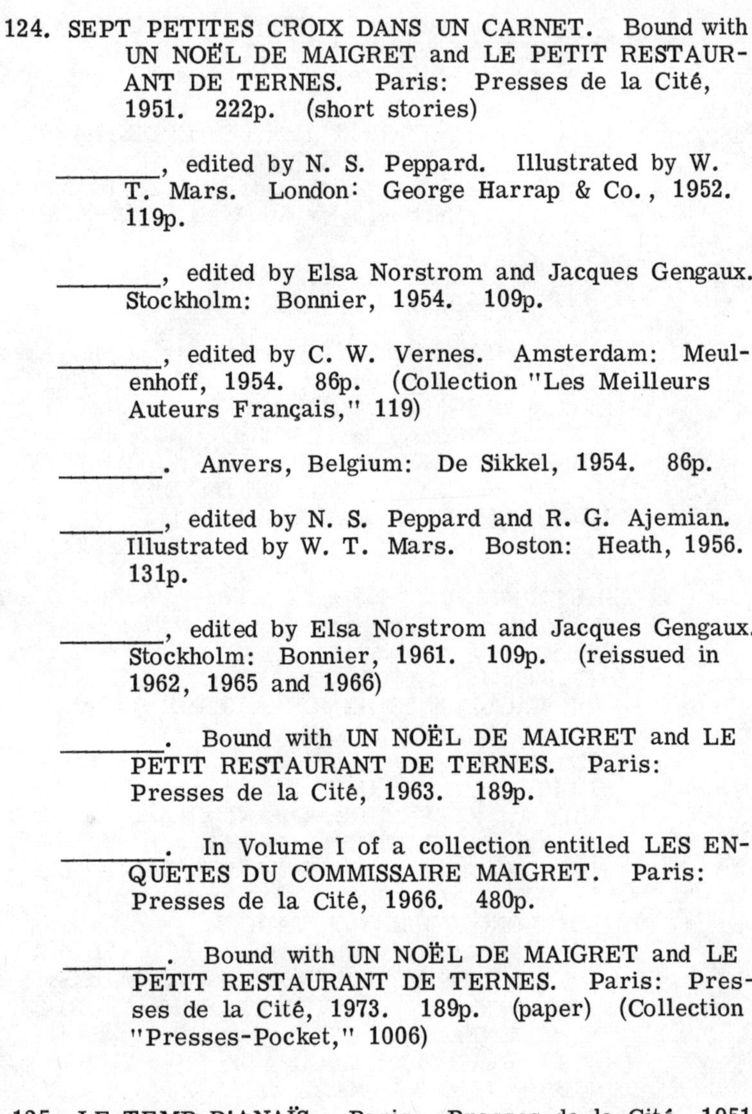

124. SEPT PETITES CROIX DANS UN CARNET. Bound with UN NOËL DE MAIGRET and LE PETIT RESTAURANT DE TERNES. Paris: Presses de la Cité, 1951. 222p. (short stories)

________, edited by N. S. Peppard. Illustrated by W. T. Mars. London: George Harrap & Co., 1952. 119p.

________, edited by Elsa Norstrom and Jacques Gengaux. Stockholm: Bonnier, 1954. 109p.

________, edited by C. W. Vernes. Amsterdam: Meulenhoff, 1954. 86p. (Collection "Les Meilleurs Auteurs Français," 119)

________. Anvers, Belgium: De Sikkel, 1954. 86p.

________, edited by N. S. Peppard and R. G. Ajemian. Illustrated by W. T. Mars. Boston: Heath, 1956. 131p.

________, edited by Elsa Norstrom and Jacques Gengaux. Stockholm: Bonnier, 1961. 109p. (reissued in 1962, 1965 and 1966)

________. Bound with UN NOËL DE MAIGRET and LE PETIT RESTAURANT DE TERNES. Paris: Presses de la Cité, 1963. 189p.

________. In Volume I of a collection entitled LES ENQUETES DU COMMISSAIRE MAIGRET. Paris: Presses de la Cité, 1966. 480p.

________. Bound with UN NOËL DE MAIGRET and LE PETIT RESTAURANT DE TERNES. Paris: Presses de la Cité, 1973. 189p. (paper) (Collection "Presses-Pocket," 1006)

125. LE TEMP D'ANAÏS. Paris: Presses de la Cité, 1951. 221p.

________. In an untitled collection with LA FUITE DE MONSIEUR MONDE and UNE VIE COMME NEUVE. Paris: Presses de la Cité, 1957. 400p. (Collection "Trio," 3)

_______. Paris: Presses de la Cité, 1964. 191p. (Collection "Simenon")

_______. Paris: Presses de la Cité, 1967. 185p. (paper) (Collection "Presses-Pocket," 509)

_______. Paris: Presses de la Cité, 1972. 215p.

English Translations
British Editions

THE GIRL IN HIS PAST, tr. by Louise Varèse. New York: Prentice-Hall, 1952. 211p.

126. UNE VIE COMME NEUVE. Paris: Presses de la Cité, 1951. 223p.

_______. Paris: Presses de la Cité, 1953. 223p.

_______. In an untitled collection with LE TEMPS D'ANAÏS and LA FUITE DE MONSIEUR MONDE. Paris: Presses de la Cité, 1957. 400p. (Collection "Trio," 3)

_______. Paris: Presses de la Cité, 1960. 253p.

_______. Paris: Presses de la Cité, 1964.

_______. Paris: Presses de la Cité, 1967. 189p. (paper) (Collection "Presses-Pocket," 535)

_______. Paris: Presses de la Cité, 1972. 192p.

English Translations
British Editions

A NEW LEASE OF LIFE, tr. by Joanna Richardson. London: Hamish Hamilton, 1963.

_______, tr. by Joanna Richardson. Harmondsworth: Penguin Books, 1966. 157p.

American Editions

A NEW LEASE ON LIFE, tr. by Joanna Richardson. Garden City, N.Y.: Doubleday, 1963. 162p.

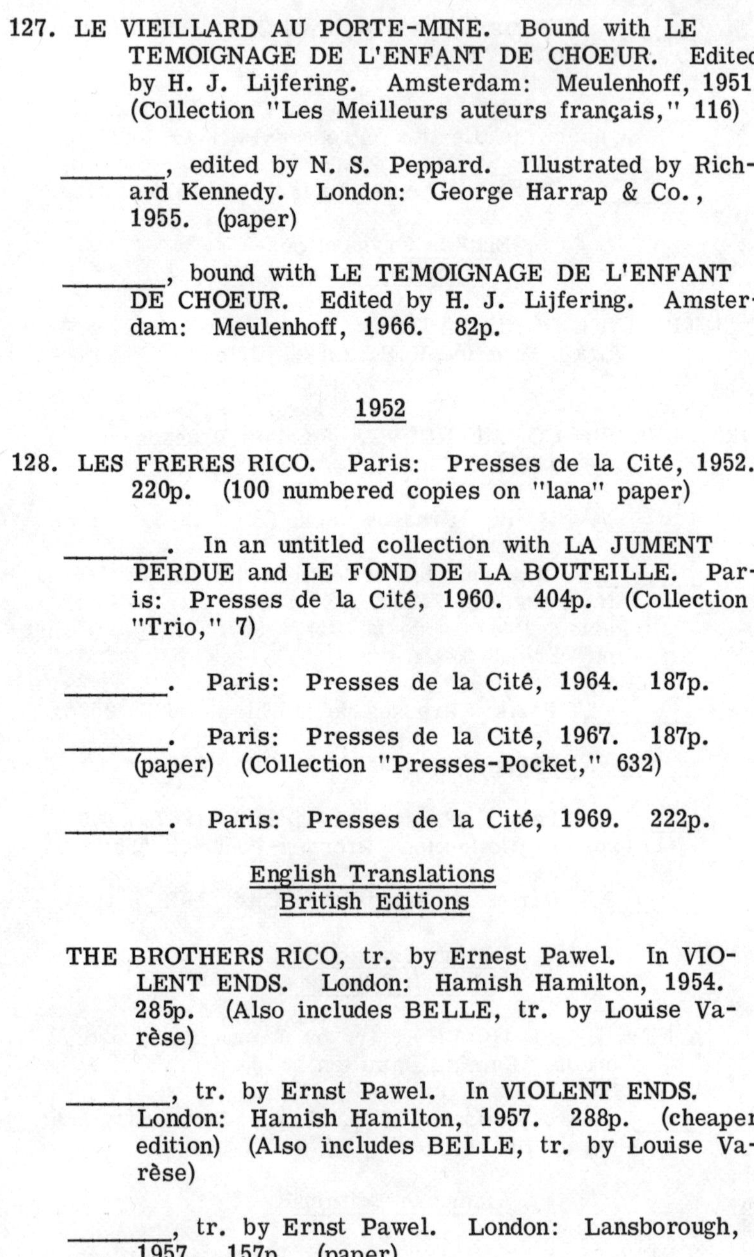

127. LE VIEILLARD AU PORTE-MINE. Bound with LE TEMOIGNAGE DE L'ENFANT DE CHOEUR. Edited by H. J. Lijfering. Amsterdam: Meulenhoff, 1951. (Collection "Les Meilleurs auteurs français," 116)

________, edited by N. S. Peppard. Illustrated by Richard Kennedy. London: George Harrap & Co., 1955. (paper)

________, bound with LE TEMOIGNAGE DE L'ENFANT DE CHOEUR. Edited by H. J. Lijfering. Amsterdam: Meulenhoff, 1966. 82p.

1952

128. LES FRERES RICO. Paris: Presses de la Cité, 1952. 220p. (100 numbered copies on "lana" paper)

________. In an untitled collection with LA JUMENT PERDUE and LE FOND DE LA BOUTEILLE. Paris: Presses de la Cité, 1960. 404p. (Collection "Trio," 7)

________. Paris: Presses de la Cité, 1964. 187p.

________. Paris: Presses de la Cité, 1967. 187p. (paper) (Collection "Presses-Pocket," 632)

________. Paris: Presses de la Cité, 1969. 222p.

English Translations
British Editions

THE BROTHERS RICO, tr. by Ernest Pawel. In VIOLENT ENDS. London: Hamish Hamilton, 1954. 285p. (Also includes BELLE, tr. by Louise Varèse)

________, tr. by Ernst Pawel. In VIOLENT ENDS. London: Hamish Hamilton, 1957. 288p. (cheaper edition) (Also includes BELLE, tr. by Louise Varèse)

________, tr. by Ernst Pawel. London: Lansborough, 1957. 157p. (paper)

________, tr. by Ernst Pawel. London: New English Library, 1966. 157p.

American Editions

________, tr. by Ernst Pawel. In a collection entitled TIDAL WAVES. Garden City, N.Y.: Doubleday, 1954. 383p. (Also includes BELLE, tr. by Louise Varèse, and THE BOTTOM OF THE BOTTLE, tr. by Cornelia Schaeffer.)

________, tr. by Ernst Pawel. In a collection entitled AN AMERICAN OMNIBUS. New York: Harcourt, Brace & World, 1967. 500p. (Also includes BELLE, THE HITCHHIKER and THE WATCHMAKER OF EVERTON)

129. LONG COURS SUR LES RIVIERES ET CANAUX. Liège: Editions Dynamo, 1952. 24p. (nonfiction)

130. MAIGRET, LOGNON ET LES GANGSTERS. Paris: Presses de la Cité, 1952. 224p. (100 numbered copies on "lana" paper)

________. Paris: Presses de la Cité, 1963. (Collection "Maigret")

________. Paris: Presses de la Cité, 1965. 190p.

English Translations
British Editions

MAIGRET AND THE GANGSTERS, tr. by Louise Varèse. London: Hamish Hamilton, 1974. 156p.

American Editions

INSPECTOR MAIGRET AND THE KILLERS, tr. by Louise Varèse. Garden City, N.Y.: Doubleday, 1954. 187p. (Published for the Crime Club)

________, tr. by Louise Varèse. New York: New American Library, 1964. 126p. (paper)

131. LA MORT DE BELLE. Paris: Presses de la Cité, 1952. 224p. (100 numbered copies on "lana" paper)

________. Paris: Presses de la Cité, 1964. 192p. (Collection "Simenon broché")

________. Paris: Presses de la Cité, 1968. 192p. (paper) (Collection "Presses-Pocket," 610)

________. Paris: Presses de la Cité, 1971. 214p.

English Translations
British Editions

BELLE, tr. by Louise Varèse. In VIOLENT ENDS. London: Hamish Hamilton, 1954. 285p. (Also includes THE BROTHERS RICO, tr. by Ernst Pawel)

________, tr. by Louise Varèse. In VIOLENT ENDS. London: Hamish Hamilton, 1957. 288p. (cheaper edition) (Also includes THE BROTHERS RICO, tr. by Ernst Pawel)

________, tr. by Louise Varèse. London: Hamilton & Co., 1958. 160p. (paper)

American Editions

________, tr. by Louise Varèse. In a collection entitled TIDAL WAVES. Garden City, N.Y.: Doubleday, 1954. 383p. (Also includes THE BROTHERS RICO, tr. by Ernst Pawel, and THE BOTTOM OF THE BOTTLE, tr. by Cornelia Schaeffer.)

________, tr. by Louise Varèse. New York: New American Library, 1954. 142p. (paper)

________, tr. by Louise Varèse. In a collection entitled AN AMERICAN OMNIBUS. New York: Harcourt, Brace & World, 1967. 500p. (Also includes THE BROTHERS RICO, THE HITCHHIKER, and THE WATCHMAKER OF EVERTON)

132. LE REVOLVER DE MAIGRET. Paris: Presses de la Cité, 1952. 218p. (100 number copies on "lana" paper)

________. Paris: Presses de la Cité, 1962. 188p.

________, edited by Herbert Collins. London: Macmillan; New York: St. Martin's Press, 1967. ix, 179p. (paper)

English Translations
British Editions

MAIGRET'S REVOLVER, tr. by Nigel Ryan. London: Hamish Hamilton, 1956. 157p.

________, tr. by Nigel Ryan. London: Hamish Hamilton, 1958. 158p. (cheaper edition)

________, tr. by Nigel Ryan. Harmondsworth: Penguin Books, 1959. 140p. (paper)

________, tr. by Nigel Ryan. In a collection entitled MAIGRET TRIUMPHANT. London: Hamish Hamilton, 1969. 507p. (Also includes MAIGRET AND THE BURGLAR'S WIFE, MY FRIEND MAIGRET, MAIGRET IN COURT and MAIGRET AFRAID)

1953

133. ANTOINE ET JULIE. Paris: Presses de la Cité, 1953. 217p.

________. Paris: Presses de la Cité, 1955. 186p.

________. In an untitled collection with L'ENTERREMENT DE MONSIEUR BOUVET and LE GRAND BOB. Paris: Presses de la Cité, 1961. 407p. (Collection "Trio," 8)

________. Paris: Presses de la Cité, 1964. 187p. (Collection "Simenon")

________. Paris: Presses de la Cité, 1969. 193p. (paper) (Collection "Presses-Pocket," 665)

________. Paris: Presses de la Cité, 1969. 224p. ("Nouvelle Collection brochée")

English Translations
British Editions

THE MAGICIAN, tr. by Helen Sebba. London: Hamish Hamilton, 1974. 188p.

American Editions

________, tr. by Helen Sebba; bound with THE WIDOW, tr. by John Petrie. Garden City, N.Y.: Doubleday, 1955. 314p.

134. L'ESCALIER DE FER. Paris: Presses de la Cité, 1953. 219p. (100 numbered copies on "lana" paper representing the original edition.)

________. Paris: Presses de la Cité, 1960.

________. Paris: Presses de la Cité, 1964. 187p.

________. Paris: Presses de la Cité, 1967. 250p. (Collection "Romans")

________. Paris: Presses de la Cité, 1969. 192p. (paper) (Collection "Presses-Pocket," 707)

________. Paris: Presses de la Cité, 1972. 250p.

English Translations
British Editions

THE IRON STAIRCASE, tr. by Eileen Ellenbogen. London: Hamish Hamilton, 1963. 158p.

________, tr. by Eileen Ellenbogen. Harmondsworth: Penguin Books, 1967. 157p. (paper)

135. FEUX ROUGES. Paris: Presses de la Cité, 1953. 221p. (100 numbered copies on "lana" paper representing the original edition.)

________. Paris: Presses de la Cité, 1961.

________. Paris: Presses de la Cité, 1964. 187p.

________. Paris: Presses de la Cité, 1969. 224p. ("Nouvelle Collection brochée")

________. Paris: Presses de la Cité, 1970. 192p. (paper) (Collection "Presses-Pocket," 753)

English Translations
British Editions

RED LIGHTS. In DANGER AHEAD, tr. by Norman Denny. London: Hamish Hamilton, 1955. 288p. (Also includes THE WATCHMAKER OF EVERTON)

________. In DANGER AHEAD, tr. by Norman Denny. London: Hamish Hamilton, 1955. 288p. (cheaper edition) (Also includes THE WATCHMAKER OF EVERTON)

________, tr. by Norman Denny. In an untitled collection with MAIGRET AND THE YOUNG GIRL and THE WATCHMAKER OF EVERTON. London: Companion Book Club, 1956. 352p.

American Editions

THE HITCHHIKER, tr. by Norman Denny. In DESTINATIONS. Garden City, N.Y.: Doubleday, 1955. 320p. (Also includes THE BURIAL OF MONSIEUR BOUVET, tr. by Eugene MacCown)

________, tr. by Norman Denny. In a collection entitled AN AMERICAN OMNIBUS. New York: Harcourt, Brace, Co., 1967. 500p. (Also includes BELLE, THE BROTHERS RICO and THE WATCHMAKER OF EVERTON)

136. MAIGRET A PEUR. Paris: Presses de la Cité, 1953. 219p. (100 numbered copies on "lana.")

________. Paris: Presses de la Cité, 1971. 188p. (paper) (Collection "Presses-Pocket," 875)

English Translations
British Editions

MAIGRET AFRAID, tr. by Margaret Duff. London:

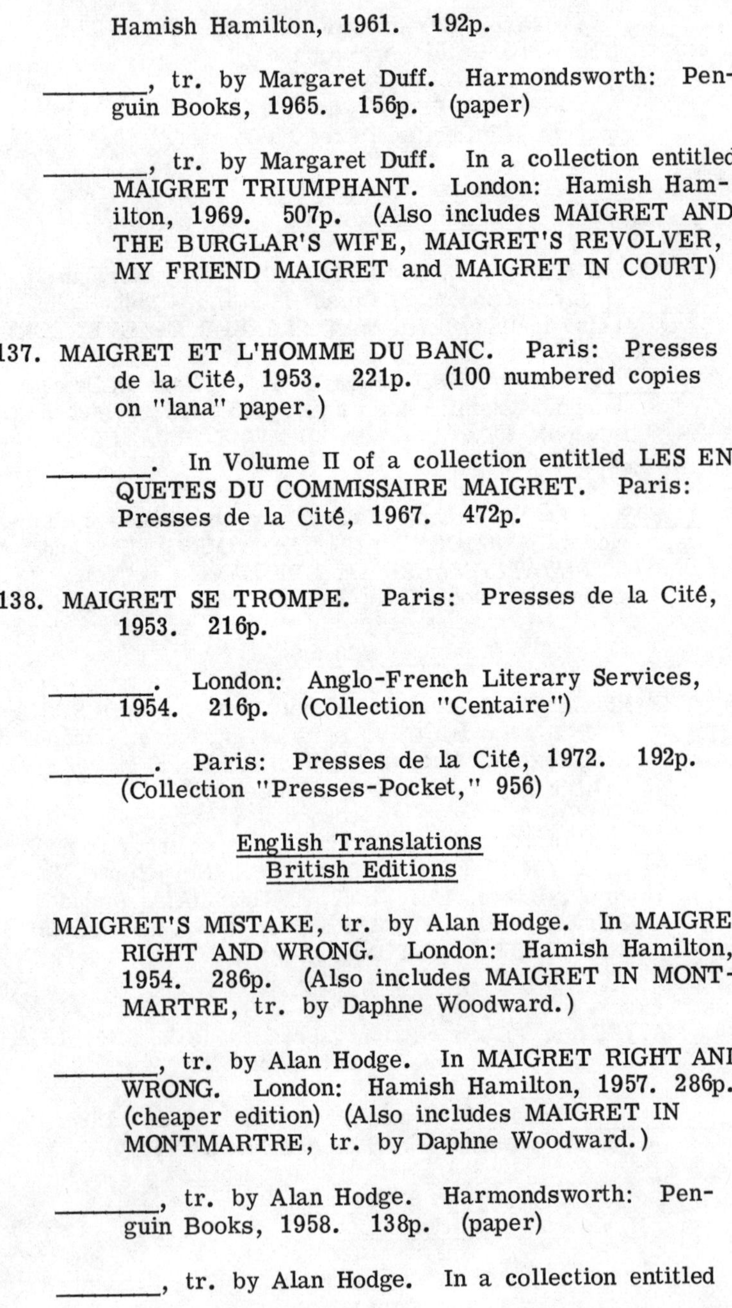

Hamish Hamilton, 1961. 192p.

________, tr. by Margaret Duff. Harmondsworth: Penguin Books, 1965. 156p. (paper)

________, tr. by Margaret Duff. In a collection entitled MAIGRET TRIUMPHANT. London: Hamish Hamilton, 1969. 507p. (Also includes MAIGRET AND THE BURGLAR'S WIFE, MAIGRET'S REVOLVER, MY FRIEND MAIGRET and MAIGRET IN COURT)

137. MAIGRET ET L'HOMME DU BANC. Paris: Presses de la Cité, 1953. 221p. (100 numbered copies on "lana" paper.)

________. In Volume II of a collection entitled LES ENQUETES DU COMMISSAIRE MAIGRET. Paris: Presses de la Cité, 1967. 472p.

138. MAIGRET SE TROMPE. Paris: Presses de la Cité, 1953. 216p.

________. London: Anglo-French Literary Services, 1954. 216p. (Collection "Centaire")

________. Paris: Presses de la Cité, 1972. 192p. (Collection "Presses-Pocket," 956)

English Translations
British Editions

MAIGRET'S MISTAKE, tr. by Alan Hodge. In MAIGRET RIGHT AND WRONG. London: Hamish Hamilton, 1954. 286p. (Also includes MAIGRET IN MONTMARTRE, tr. by Daphne Woodward.)

________, tr. by Alan Hodge. In MAIGRET RIGHT AND WRONG. London: Hamish Hamilton, 1957. 286p. (cheaper edition) (Also includes MAIGRET IN MONTMARTRE, tr. by Daphne Woodward.)

________, tr. by Alan Hodge. Harmondsworth: Penguin Books, 1958. 138p. (paper)

________, tr. by Alan Hodge. In a collection entitled

A MAIGRET OMNIBUS. London: Hamish Hamilton, 1962. 525p. (Also includes MAIGRET IN MONTMARTRE, MAIGRET AND THE RELUCTANT WITNESSES and MAIGRET GOES TO SCHOOL.)

________, tr. by Alan Hodge. In MAIGRET RIGHT AND WRONG. London: Hamish Hamilton, 1967. 286p. (Also includes MAIGRET IN MONTMARTRE, tr. by Daphne Woodward.)

American Editions

________, tr. by Alan Hodge. In a collection entitled FIVE TIMES MAIGRET. New York: Harcourt, Brace & Co., 1964. 525p. (Same contents as A MAIGRET OMNIBUS.)

1954

139. LE BATEAU D'EMILE. Paris: Gallimard, 1954. 240p. (50 copies on finer paper, representing the original edition.) (Also includes LA FEMME DU PILOTE, LE DOIGT DE BARRAQUIER, VALERIE S'EN VA, L'EPINGLE EN FER A CHEVAL, LE BARON DE L'ECLUSE OR, LA CROISIERE DU "POTAM," LE NEGRE S'EST ENDORMI, LE DUEL DE FONSINE, L'HOMME A BARBE.)

________. Paris: Gallimard, 1968. 237p. (Same contents as main entry)

140. CRIME IMPUNI. Paris: Presses de la Cité, 1954. 222p. (100 copies on "alfa" paper)

________. Paris: Presses de la Cité, 1964. 187p. (Collection "Simenon")

________. Paris: Presses de la Cité, 1966. 256p.

________. Paris: Presses de la Cité, 1971. 219p.

________. Paris: Presses de la Cité, 1974. (Collection "Simenon broché")

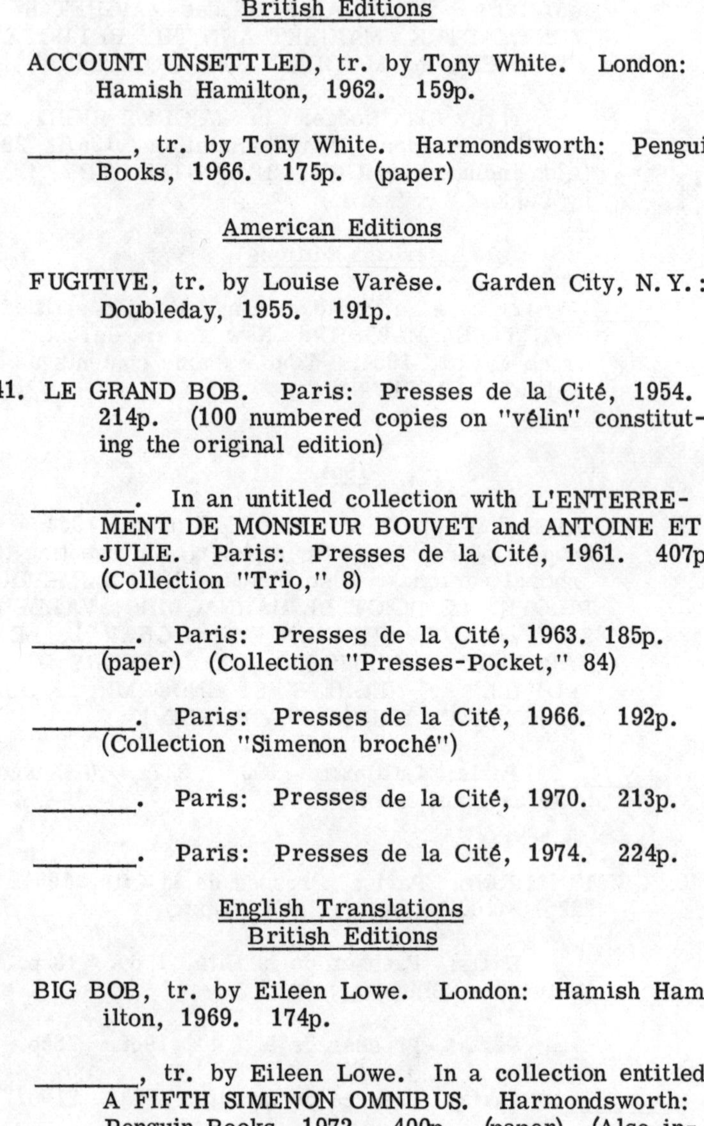

English Translations
British Editions

ACCOUNT UNSETTLED, tr. by Tony White. London: Hamish Hamilton, 1962. 159p.

________, tr. by Tony White. Harmondsworth: Penguin Books, 1966. 175p. (paper)

American Editions

FUGITIVE, tr. by Louise Varèse. Garden City, N.Y.: Doubleday, 1955. 191p.

141. LE GRAND BOB. Paris: Presses de la Cité, 1954. 214p. (100 numbered copies on "vélin" constituting the original edition)

________. In an untitled collection with L'ENTERREMENT DE MONSIEUR BOUVET and ANTOINE ET JULIE. Paris: Presses de la Cité, 1961. 407p. (Collection "Trio," 8)

________. Paris: Presses de la Cité, 1963. 185p. (paper) (Collection "Presses-Pocket," 84)

________. Paris: Presses de la Cité, 1966. 192p. (Collection "Simenon broché")

________. Paris: Presses de la Cité, 1970. 213p.

________. Paris: Presses de la Cité, 1974. 224p.

English Translations
British Editions

BIG BOB, tr. by Eileen Lowe. London: Hamish Hamilton, 1969. 174p.

________, tr. by Eileen Lowe. In a collection entitled A FIFTH SIMENON OMNIBUS. Harmondsworth: Penguin Books, 1972. 400p. (paper) (Also includes MAIGRET'S BOYHOOD FRIEND and NOVEMBER)

142. L'HORLOGER D'EVERTON. Paris: Presses de la Cité, 1954. 216p. (100 numbered copies on "vélin," constituting the original edition)

_______. Paris: Presses de la Cité, 1965. 187p.

_______. Paris: Presses de la Cité, 1966. 256p. (Collection "Romans")

_______. Paris: Presses de la Cité, 1971. 189p. (paper) (Collection "Presses-Pocket," 841)

_______. Paris: Presses de la Cité, 1971. 224p.

English Translations
British Editions

THE WATCHMAKER OF EVERTON. In DANGER AHEAD, tr. by Norman Denny. London: Hamish Hamilton, 1955. 288p. (Also includes RED LIGHTS)

_______. In DANGER AHEAD, tr. by Norman Denny. London: Hamish Hamilton, 1955. 288p. (cheaper edition). (Also includes RED LIGHTS)

_______, tr. by Norman Denny. In an untitled collection with MAIGRET AND THE YOUNG GIRL and RED LIGHTS. London: Companion Book Club, 1956. 352p.

American Editions

_______, tr. by Norman Denny. Bound with WITNESSES, tr. by Moura Budberg. Garden City, N.Y.: Doubleday, 1956. 315p.

_______, tr. by Norman Denny. In a collection entitled AN AMERICAN OMNIBUS. New York: Harcourt, Brace & World, 1967. 500p. (Also includes BELLE, THE BROTHERS RICO and THE HITCH-HIKER.)

143. MAIGRET A L'ECOLE. Paris: Presses de la Cité, 1954. 224p. (100 numbered copies on "vélin" representing the original edition.)

English Translations
British Editions

MAIGRET GOES TO SCHOOL, tr. by Daphne Woodward. London: Hamish Hamilton, 1957. 157p.

________, tr. by Daphne Woodward. London: Hamish Hamilton, 1959. 160p. (cheaper edition).

________, tr. by Daphne Woodward. London: Landsborough, 1960. 160p. (paper)

________, tr. by Daphne Woodward. London: New English Library, 1962. (paper) (reissued in 1965)

________, tr. by Daphne Woodward. In a collection entitled A MAIGRET OMNIBUS. London: Hamish Hamilton, 1962. 525p. (Also includes MAIGRET IN MONTMARTRE, MAIGRET'S MISTAKE, MAIGRET HAS SCRUPLES and MAIGRET AND THE RELUCTANT WITNESSES)

American Editions

________, tr. by Daphne Woodward. In a collection entitled FIVE TIMES MAIGRET. New York: Harcourt, Brace & Co., 1964. 525p. (Same contents as A MAIGRET OMNIBUS)

144. MAIGRET CHEZ LE MINISTRE. Lakeville, Connecticut, 1954. 230p. (100 numbered mimeograph copies which represent the original edition.)

________. Paris: Presses de la Cité, 1955. 220p. (100 numbered copies on "vélin" paper.)

________. Paris: Presses de la Cité, 1957. 220p.

________. Paris: Presses de la Cité, 1972. 190p. (paper) (Collection "Presses Pocket," 946)

English Translations
British Editions

MAIGRET AND THE MINISTER, tr. by Moura Budberg. London: Hamish Hamilton, 1969. 175p.

_______, tr. by Moura Budberg. In a collection entitled THE THIRD MAIGRET OMNIBUS. Harmondsworth: Penguin Books, 1971. 366p. (paper) (Also includes MAIGRET HAS DOUBTS and THE OLD MAN DIES)

American Editions

MAIGRET AND THE CALAME REPORT, tr. by Moura Budberg. New York: Harcourt, Brace & World, 1969. 183p.

145. MAIGRET ET LA JEUNE MORTE. Paris: Presses de la Cité, 1954. 221p.

English Translations
British Editions

MAIGRET AND THE YOUNG GIRL, tr. by Daphne Woodward. London: Hamish Hamilton, 1955. 159p.

_______. tr. by Daphne Woodward. Bound with RED LIGHTS and THE WATCHMAKER OF EVERTON. London: Companion Book Club, 1956. 352p.

_______, tr. by Daphne Woodward. London: Hamish Hamilton, 1957. 160p. (cheaper edition)

_______, tr. by Daphne Woodward. London: Hutchinson, 1958. 192p. (paper)

_______, tr. by Daphne Woodward. In a collection entitled THE SECOND MAIGRET OMNIBUS. London: Hamish Hamilton, 1964. 523p. (Also includes MAIGRET'S LITTLE JOKE, MAIGRET AND THE OLD LADY, MAIGRET'S FIRST CASE and MAIGRET TAKES A ROOM)

_______, tr. by Daphne Woodward. London: Arrow Books, 1965. 191p. (paper)

_______, tr. by Daphne Woodward. Leicester: Thorpe, 1967. 184p. (Ulverscroft large print series)

American Editions

INSPECTOR MAIGRET AND THE DEAD GIRL, tr. by Daphne Woodward. Garden City, N.Y.: Doubleday, 1955. 192p. (Published for the Crime Club)

MAIGRET AND THE YOUNG GIRL, tr. by Daphne Woodward. In an untitled collection with THE LONG BODY by Helen McCloy, and ENOUGH TO KILL A HORSE by E. X. Ferrors. Roslyn, N.Y.: W. J. Black, 1955. 424p.

________, tr. by Daphne Woodward. In a collection entitled MAIGRET CINQ. New York: Harcourt, Brace & Co., 1965. 523p. (Same contents as THE SECOND MAIGRET OMNIBUS)

146. LES TEMOINS. Lakeville, Conn., 1954. 231p. (100 numbered copies mimeographed by the author which constitute the original edition.)

________. Paris: Presses de la Cité, 1955. 215p.

________. Paris: Presses de la Cité, 1960.

________. Paris: Presses de la Cité, 1961. 251p. (Collection "Georges Simenon")

________. Paris: Presses de la Cité, 1965. 187p.

________. Paris: Presses de la Cité, 1970. 224p. (Collection "Simenon broché")

________. Paris: Presses de la Cité, 1974. 189p. (paper) (Collection "Presses-Pocket," 1082)

English Translations
British Editions

THE WITNESSES, tr. by Moura Budberg. In THE JUDGE AND THE HATTER. London: Hamish Hamilton, 1956. 308p. (Also includes THE HATTER'S GHOST, tr. by Nigel Ryan)

________, tr. by Moura Budberg. In THE JUDGE AND THE HATTER. London: Hamish Hamilton 1958.

308p. (cheaper edition)

________, tr. by Moura Budberg. London: Landsborough, 1958. 159p. (paper)

________, tr. by Moura Budberg. London: New English Library, 1966. 157p. (paper) (reissued in 1968)

________, tr. by Moura Budberg. London: White Lion, 1974. 154p.

American Editions

________, tr. by Moura Budberg. Bound with THE WATCHMAKER OF EVERTON, tr. by Norman Denny. Garden City, N.Y.: Doubleday, 1956. 315p.

1955

147. LA BOULE NOIRE. Lakeville, Conn., 1955. (100 numbered mimeograph copies which represent the original edition.)

________. Paris: Presses de la Cité, 1955. 215p.

________. Paris: Presses de la Cité, 1965. 185p.

________. Paris: Presses de la Cité, 1966. 256p. (Collection "Romans")

________. Paris: Presses de la Cité, 1970. 180p. (paper) (Collection "Presses-Pocket," 776)

________. Paris: Presses de la Cité, 1971. 248p.

148. LES COMPLICES. Paris: Presses de la Cité, 1955. 218p. (100 numbered copies on "alfa" paper.)

________. Paris: Presses de la Cité, 1965. 187p.

________. Paris: Presses de la Cité, 1970. 224p. (Collection "Simenon broché")

________. Paris: Presses de la Cité, 1973. 185p.

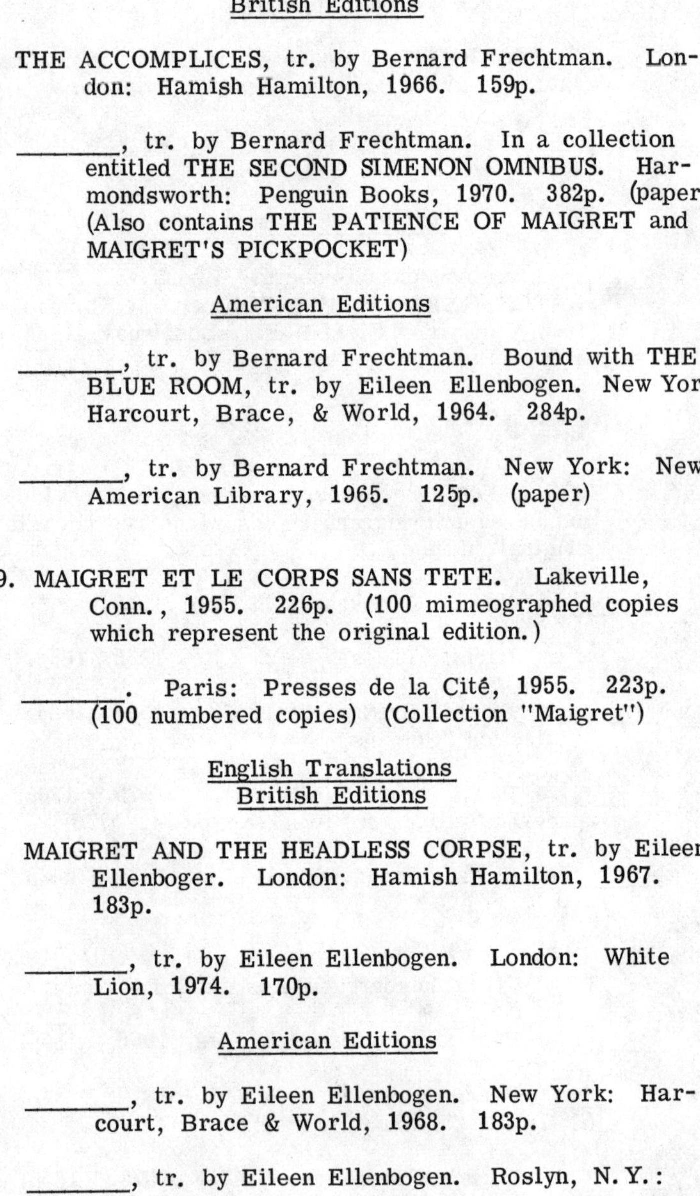

(paper) (Collection "Presses-Pocket," 1014)

English Translations
British Editions

THE ACCOMPLICES, tr. by Bernard Frechtman. London: Hamish Hamilton, 1966. 159p.

________, tr. by Bernard Frechtman. In a collection entitled THE SECOND SIMENON OMNIBUS. Harmondsworth: Penguin Books, 1970. 382p. (paper) (Also contains THE PATIENCE OF MAIGRET and MAIGRET'S PICKPOCKET)

American Editions

________, tr. by Bernard Frechtman. Bound with THE BLUE ROOM, tr. by Eileen Ellenbogen. New York: Harcourt, Brace, & World, 1964. 284p.

________, tr. by Bernard Frechtman. New York: New American Library, 1965. 125p. (paper)

149. MAIGRET ET LE CORPS SANS TETE. Lakeville, Conn., 1955. 226p. (100 mimeographed copies which represent the original edition.)

________. Paris: Presses de la Cité, 1955. 223p. (100 numbered copies) (Collection "Maigret")

English Translations
British Editions

MAIGRET AND THE HEADLESS CORPSE, tr. by Eileen Ellenboger. London: Hamish Hamilton, 1967. 183p.

________, tr. by Eileen Ellenbogen. London: White Lion, 1974. 170p.

American Editions

________, tr. by Eileen Ellenbogen. New York: Harcourt, Brace & World, 1968. 183p.

________, tr. by Eileen Ellenbogen. Roslyn, N.Y.:

Detective Book Club, 1968. 134p.

150. MAIGRET TEND UN PIEGE. Paris: Presses de la Cité, 1955. 187p.

________. Paris: Presses de la Cité, 1965. 185p.

________. Paris: Presses de la Cité, 1967. 187p.

________. Adaptation in easy French. Paris: Hachette, 1973. 95p.

English Translations
British Editions

MAIGRET SETS A TRAP, tr. by Daphne Woodward. London: Hamish Hamilton, 1965. 144p.

________, tr. by Daphne Woodward. Harmondsworth: Penguin Books, 1968. 140p. (paper)

American Editions

________, tr. by Daphne Woodward. New York: Harcourt, Brace & World, 1972. 182p. (Helen and Kurt Wolff book)

________, tr. by Daphne Woodward. New York: Curtis Books, 1973. 190p. (paper)

1956

151. UN ECHEC DE MAIGRET. Paris: Presses de la Cité, 1956. 184p. (100 numbered copies which constitute the original edition.)

English Translations
British Editions

MAIGRET'S FAILURE, tr. by Daphne Woodward. London: Hamish Hamilton, 1962. 153p.

________, tr. by Daphne Woodward. Harmondsworth: Penguin Books, 1965. 159p. (paper)

________, tr. by Daphne Woodward. In a collection entitled A MAIGRET QUARTET. London: Hamish Hamilton, 1972. 416p. (Also includes MAIGRET IN SOCIETY, MAIGRET AND THE LAZY BURGLAR and MAIGRET'S SPECIAL MURDER)

American Editions

________, tr. by Daphne Woodward. In a collection entitled A MAIGRET TRIO. New York: Harcourt, Brace & World, 1973. 290p. (Also includes MAIGRET IN SOCIETY and MAIGRET'S SPECIAL MURDER)

152. EN CAS DE MALHEUR. Paris: Presses de la Cité, 1956. 221p. (100 numbered copies which constitute the original edition.)

________. Paris: Presses de la Cité, 1965. 187p.

________. Paris: Presses de la Cité, 1970. 222p.

________. Paris: Presses de la Cité, 1973. 188p. (paper) (Collection "Presses-Pocket," 1028)

English Translations
British Editions

IN CASE OF EMERGENCY, tr. by Helen Sebba. London: Hamish Hamilton, 1960. 184p.

________, tr. by Helen Sebba. Harmondsworth: Penguin Books, 1965. 157p. (paper)

________, tr. by Helen Sebba. In a collection entitled A SIMENON OMNIBUS. London: Hamish Hamilton, 1965. 503p. (Also includes MR. HIRE'S ENGAGEMENT, SUNDAY, THE LITTLE MAN FROM ARCHANGEL and THE PREMIER)

American Editions

________, tr. by Helen Sebba. Garden City, N.Y.: Doubleday, 1958.

________, tr. by Helen Sebba. New York: MacFadden,

1964. 143p. (paper)

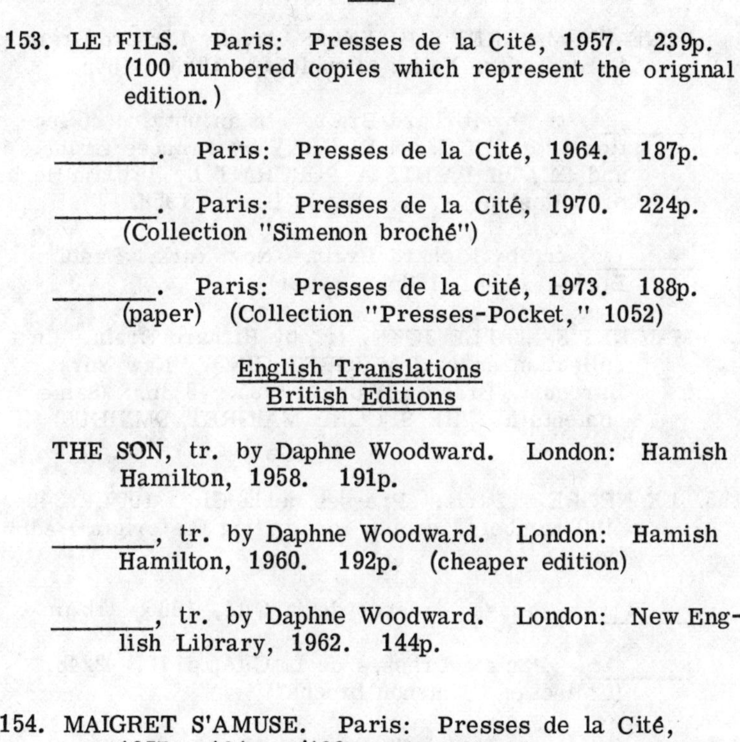

1957

153. LE FILS. Paris: Presses de la Cité, 1957. 239p. (100 numbered copies which represent the original edition.)

________. Paris: Presses de la Cité, 1964. 187p.

________. Paris: Presses de la Cité, 1970. 224p. (Collection "Simenon broché")

________. Paris: Presses de la Cité, 1973. 188p. (paper) (Collection "Presses-Pocket," 1052)

English Translations
British Editions

THE SON, tr. by Daphne Woodward. London: Hamish Hamilton, 1958. 191p.

________, tr. by Daphne Woodward. London: Hamish Hamilton, 1960. 192p. (cheaper edition)

________, tr. by Daphne Woodward. London: New English Library, 1962. 144p.

154. MAIGRET S'AMUSE. Paris: Presses de la Cité, 1957. 184p. (100 numbered copies representing the original edition.)

English Translations
British Editions

MAIGRET'S LITTLE JOKE, tr. by Richard Brain. London: Hamish Hamilton, 1957. 160p.

________, tr. by Richard Brain. London: Arrow Books, 1961. 160p. (paper)

________, tr. by Richard Brain. In a collection entitled THE SECOND MAIGRET OMNIBUS. London: Hamish Hamilton, 1964. 523p. (Also includes MAIGRET AND THE YOUNG GIRL, MAIGRET AND

THE OLD LADY, MAIGRET'S FIRST CASE and MAIGRET TAKES A ROOM)

American Editions

NONE OF MAIGRET'S BUSINESS, tr. by Richard Brain. Garden City, N.Y.: Doubleday, 1958. 184p.

________, tr. by Richard Brain. In an untitled collection with THE MAN IN GRAY by Frances Crane, and DEATH PAINTS A PORTRAIT by William Herber. Roslyn, N.Y.: W. J. Black, 1958.

________, tr. by Richard Brain. New York: Bantam Books, 1960. 120p. (paper)

MAIGRET'S LITTLE JOKE, tr. by Richard Brain. In a collection entitled MAIGRET CINQ. New York: Harcourt, Brace & World, 1965. 523p. (Same contents as THE SECOND MAIGRET OMNIBUS)

155. LE NEGRE. Paris: Presses de la Cité, 1957. 240p. (100 numbered copies constituting the original edition.)

________. Paris: Presses de la Cité, 1965. 187p.

________. Paris: Presses de la Cité, 1970. 224p. (Collection "Simenon broché")

English Translations
British Editions

THE NEGRO, tr. by Helen Sebba. London: Hamish Hamilton, 1959. 191p.

________, tr. by Helen Sebba. London: Hamish Hamilton, 1961. 192p. (cheaper edition)

________, tr. by Helen Sebba. London: New English Library, 1962. (paper)

156. LE PETIT HOMME D'ARKHANGELSK. Paris: Presses de la Cité, 1957. 219p. (100 numbered copies on "alfa" paper representing the original edition.)

________. Paris: Presses de la Cité, 1964. 251p. (Collection "Romans")

________. Paris: Presses de la Cité, 1967. 192p. (Collection "Simenon broché")

________. Paris: Presses de la Cité, 1971. 214p.

________. Paris: Presses de la Cité, 1974.

English Translations
British Editions

THE LITTLE MAN FROM ARCHANGEL, tr. by Nigel Ryan. London: Hamish Hamilton, 1957. 159p.

________, tr. by Nigel Ryan. London: Hamish Hamilton, 1959. 160p. (cheaper edition)

________, tr. by Nigel Ryan. Harmondsworth: Penguin Books, 1964. 159p. (paper)

________, tr. by Nigel Ryan. In a collection entitled A SIMENON OMNIBUS. London: Hamish Hamilton, 1965. 503p. (Also includes MR. HIRE'S ENGAGEMENT, IN CASE OF EMERGENCY, SUNDAY and THE PREMIER)

American Editions

________, tr. by Nigel Ryan. Bound with SUNDAY. New York: Harcourt, Brace & World, 1966. 267p.

1958

157. MAIGRET VOYAGE. Paris: Presses de la Cité, 1958. 320p. (Collection "Maigret")

English Translations
British Editions

MAIGRET AND THE MILLIONAIRES, tr. by Jean Stewart. London: Hamish Hamilton, 1974. 156p.

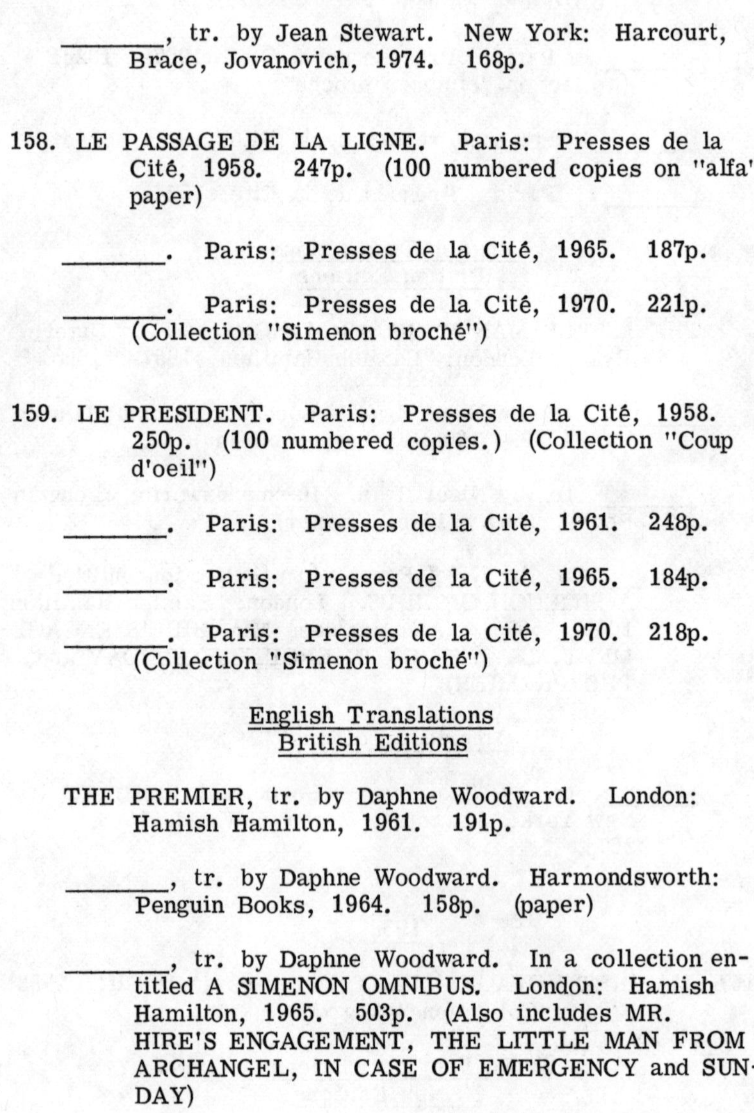

American Editions

________, tr. by Jean Stewart. New York: Harcourt, Brace, Jovanovich, 1974. 168p.

158. LE PASSAGE DE LA LIGNE. Paris: Presses de la Cité, 1958. 247p. (100 numbered copies on "alfa" paper)

________. Paris: Presses de la Cité, 1965. 187p.

________. Paris: Presses de la Cité, 1970. 221p. (Collection "Simenon broché")

159. LE PRESIDENT. Paris: Presses de la Cité, 1958. 250p. (100 numbered copies.) (Collection "Coup d'oeil")

________. Paris: Presses de la Cité, 1961. 248p.

________. Paris: Presses de la Cité, 1965. 184p.

________. Paris: Presses de la Cité, 1970. 218p. (Collection "Simenon broché")

English Translations
British Editions

THE PREMIER, tr. by Daphne Woodward. London: Hamish Hamilton, 1961. 191p.

________, tr. by Daphne Woodward. Harmondsworth: Penguin Books, 1964. 158p. (paper)

________, tr. by Daphne Woodward. In a collection entitled A SIMENON OMNIBUS. London: Hamish Hamilton, 1965. 503p. (Also includes MR. HIRE'S ENGAGEMENT, THE LITTLE MAN FROM ARCHANGEL, IN CASE OF EMERGENCY and SUNDAY)

American Editions

________, tr. by Daphne Woodward. Bound with THE TRAIN, tr. by Robert Baldick. New York: Harcourt, Brace & World, 1966. 248p.

_______, tr. by Daphne Woodward. New York: Pocket Books, 1968. 160p. (paper)

160. LES SCRUPULES DE MAIGRET. Paris: Presses de la Cité, 1958. 192p. (100 numbered copies which constitute the original edition.)

_______. Paris: Presses de la Cité, 1970. 184p. (paper) (Collection "Presses-Pocket," 808)

English Translations
British Editions

MAIGRET HAS SCRUPLES, tr. by Robert Eglesfield. London: Hamish Hamilton, 1959. 183p.

_______, tr. by Robert Eglesfield. London: Hamish Hamilton, 1961. 184p. (cheaper edition)

_______, tr. by Robert Eglesfield. Harmondsworth: Penguin Books, 1962. 127p. (paper)

_______, tr. by Robert Eglesfield. In a collection entitled A MAIGRET OMNIBUS. London: Hamish Hamilton, 1962. 525p. (Also includes MAIGRET RIGHT AND WRONG, MAIGRET IN MONTMARTRE, MAIGRET'S MISTAKE, MAIGRET AND THE RELUCTANT WITNESSES and MAIGRET GOES TO SCHOOL)

American Editions

_______, tr. by Robert Eglesfield. In VERSUS INSPECTOR MAIGRET. Garden City, N.Y.: Doubleday, 1960. 239p. (Also includes MAIGRET AND THE RELUCTANT WITNESSES, tr. by Daphne Woodward)

_______, tr. by Robert Eglesfield. Bound with MAIGRET AND THE RELUCTANT WITNESSES, tr. by Daphne Woodward. New York: Ace, 1962. 128p. (paper)

_______, tr. by Robert Eglesfield. In a collection entitled FIVE TIMES MAIGRET. New York: Harcourt, Brace & World, 1964. 525p. (Same contents as A MAIGRET OMNIBUS)

161. STRIP-TEASE. Paris: Presses de la Cité, 1958. 242p. (100 numbered copies representing the original edition)

________. Paris: Presses de la Cité, 1965. 187p.

________. Paris: Presses de la Cité, 1969. 228p. (Collection "Simenon broché")

________. Paris: Presses de la Cité, 1973. 188p. (paper) (Collection "Presses-Pocket," 972)

English Translations
British Editions

STRIPTEASE, tr. by Robert Brain. London: Hamish Hamilton, 1959. 189p.

________, tr. by Robert Brain. Harmondsworth: Penguin Books, 1963. 142p. (paper)

________, tr. by Robert Brain. In a collection entitled THE SECOND SIMENON OMNIBUS. London: Hamish Hamilton, 1974. 480p. (Also includes CHEZ KRULL, THE HEART OF A MAN and THE WIDOWER)

1959

162. UNE CONFIDENCE DE MAIGRET. Paris: Presses de la Cité, 1959. 189p. (100 numbered copies constituting the original edition)

________. Paris: Presses de la Cité, 1959. 226p. (Collection "Cavalcade")

________. Paris: Presses de la Cité, 1971. 188p.

English Translations
British Editions

MAIGRET HAS DOUBTS, tr. by Lyn Moir. London:

Hamish Hamilton, 1968. 138p.

________, tr. by Lyn Moir. In a collection entitled THE THIRD MAIGRET OMNIBUS. Harmondsworth: Penguin Books, 1971. 336p. (paper) (Also includes THE OLD MAN DIES and MAIGRET AND THE MINISTER)

________, tr. by Lyn Moir. London: White Lion, 1974. 138p. (paper)

163. DIMANCHE. Paris: Presses de la Cité, 1959. 244p. (100 numbered "de luxe" copies constituting the original edition.)

________. Paris: Presses de la Cité, 1959. 226p.

________. Paris: Presses de la Cité, 1965. 186p.

________. Paris: Presses de la Cité, 1970. 219p. (Collection "Simenon broché")

English Translations
British Editions

SUNDAY, tr. by Nigel Ryan. London: Hamish Hamilton, 1960. 191p.

________, tr. by Nigel Ryan. Harmondsworth: Penguin Books, 1963. 135p. (paper)

________, tr. by Nigel Ryan. In a collection entitled A SIMENON OMNIBUS. London: Hamish Hamilton, 1965. 503p. (Also includes MR. HIRE'S ENGAGEMENT, THE LITTLE MAN FROM ARCHANGEL, IN CASE OF EMERGENCY and THE PREMIER)

American Editions

________, tr. by Nigel Ryan. Bound with THE LITTLE MAN FROM ARCHANGEL. New York: Harcourt, Brace & World, 1966. 267p.

164. MAIGRET ET LES TEMOINS RECALCITRANTS.

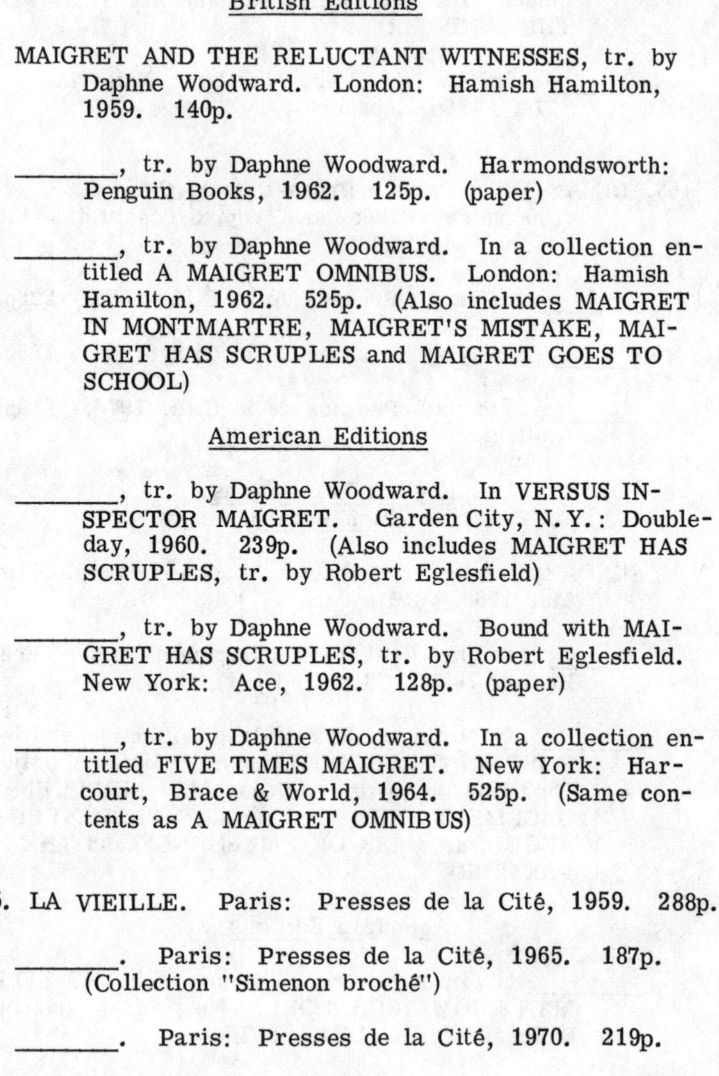

Paris: Presses de la Cité, 1959. 192p. (100 numbered "de luxe" copies constituting the original edition.)

English Translations
British Editions

MAIGRET AND THE RELUCTANT WITNESSES, tr. by Daphne Woodward. London: Hamish Hamilton, 1959. 140p.

________, tr. by Daphne Woodward. Harmondsworth: Penguin Books, 1962. 125p. (paper)

________, tr. by Daphne Woodward. In a collection entitled A MAIGRET OMNIBUS. London: Hamish Hamilton, 1962. 525p. (Also includes MAIGRET IN MONTMARTRE, MAIGRET'S MISTAKE, MAIGRET HAS SCRUPLES and MAIGRET GOES TO SCHOOL)

American Editions

________, tr. by Daphne Woodward. In VERSUS INSPECTOR MAIGRET. Garden City, N.Y.: Doubleday, 1960. 239p. (Also includes MAIGRET HAS SCRUPLES, tr. by Robert Eglesfield)

________, tr. by Daphne Woodward. Bound with MAIGRET HAS SCRUPLES, tr. by Robert Eglesfield. New York: Ace, 1962. 128p. (paper)

________, tr. by Daphne Woodward. In a collection entitled FIVE TIMES MAIGRET. New York: Harcourt, Brace & World, 1964. 525p. (Same contents as A MAIGRET OMNIBUS)

165. LA VIEILLE. Paris: Presses de la Cité, 1959. 288p.

________. Paris: Presses de la Cité, 1965. 187p. (Collection "Simenon broché")

________. Paris: Presses de la Cité, 1970. 219p.

Titles First Published in the 1960s

1960

166. LA FEMME EN FRANCE. Paris: Presses de la Cité, 1960. (Non-fiction. Photographer: Danièle Frasney)

167. MAIGRET AUX ASSISES. Paris: Presses de la Cité, 1960. 190p. (100 numbered copies)

English Translations
British Editions

MAIGRET IN COURT, tr. by Robert Brain. London: Hamish Hamilton, 1961. 192p.

________, tr. by Robert Brain. Harmondsworth: Penguin Books, 1965. 110p. (paper)

________, tr. by Robert Brain. In a collection entitled MAIGRET TRIUMPHANT. London: Hamish Hamilton, 1969. 507p. (Also includes MAIGRET AND THE BURGLAR'S WIFE, MAIGRET'S REVOLVER, MY FRIEND MAIGRET and MAIGRET AFRAID)

168. MAIGRET ET LES VIEILLARDS. Paris: Presses de la Cité, 1960. (Collection "Maigret")

English Translations
British Editions

MAIGRET IN SOCIETY, tr. by Robert Eglesfield. London: Hamish Hamilton, 1962. 160p.

________, tr. by Robert Eglesfield. Harmondsworth: Penguin Books, 1965. 135p. (paper)

________, tr. by Robert Eglesfield. Leicester: F. A. Thorpe, 1965. 160p. (Ulverscroft large print series)

________, tr. by Robert Eglesfield. In a collection entitled A MAIGRET QUARTET. London: Hamish Hamilton, 1972. 416p. (Also includes MAIGRET'S FAILURE, MAIGRET AND THE LAZY BURGLAR and MAIGRET'S SPECIAL MURDER)

American Editions

________, tr. by Robert Eglesfield. In a collection entitled A MAIGRET TRIO. New York: Harcourt Brace Jovanovich, 1973. 290p. (Also includes MAIGRET'S FAILURE and MAIGRET AND THE LAZY BURGLAR)

169. L'OURS EN PELUCHE. Paris: Presses de la Cité, 1960. 230p. (also "de luxe" edition) (Collection "Psychologique")

________. Paris: Presses de la Cité, 1965. 187p. (Collection "Simenon broché")

________. Paris: Presses de la Cité, 1970. 216p.

English Translations
British Editions

TEDDY BEAR, tr. by John Clay. London: Hamish Hamilton, 1971. 156p.

American Editions

________, tr. by John Clay. New York: Harcourt Brace Jovanovich, 1972. 162p.

170. LE ROMAN DE L'HOMME. Paris: Presses de la Cité, 1960. 93p. (Lecture delivered at The Brussels World's Fair, October 3, 1958.) (Nonfiction)

English Translations
American Editions

THE NOVEL OF A MAN, tr. by Bernard Frechtman. New York: Harcourt, Brace & World, 1964. 59p.

171. LE VEUF. Paris: Presses de la Cité, 1960. 252p. (Collection "Simenon")

________. Paris: Presses de la Cité, 1965. 187p. (Collection "Simenon broché")

________. Paris: Presses de la Cité, 1970. 218p.

English Translations
British Editions

THE WIDOWER, tr. by Robert Baldick. London: Hamish Hamilton, 1961. 191p.

________, tr. by Robert Baldick. Harmondsworth: Penguin Books, 1965. 142p. (paper)

________, tr. by Robert Baldick. In a collection entitled THE SECOND SIMENON OMNIBUS. London: Hamish Hamilton, 1974. 480p. (Also includes CHEZ KRULL, THE HEART OF A MAN and STRIPTEASE)

1961

172. BETTY. Paris: Presses de la Cité, 1961. 220p.

________. Paris: Presses de la Cité, 1965. 187p.

________. Paris: Presses de la Cité, 1970. 212p. (Collection "Simenon broché")

English Translations
British Editions

BETTY, tr. by Alastair Hamilton. London: Hamish Hamilton, 1975. 124p.

American Editions

________, tr. by Alastair Hamilton. New York: Harcourt Brace Jovanovich, 1975. 165p.

173. MAIGRET ET LE VOLEUR PARESSEUX. Paris: Presses de la Cité, 1961. 187p. (Collection "Maigret")

________. Paris: Presses de la Cité, 1970. 192p. (paper) (Collection "Presses-Pocket," 807)

________. Paris: Presses de la Cité, 1972. 192p.

English Translations
British Editions

MAIGRET AND THE LAZY BURGLAR, tr. by Daphne Woodward. London: Hamish Hamilton, 1963. 140p.

________, tr. by Daphne Woodward. Harmondsworth: Penguin Books, 1966. 142p. (paper)

________, tr. by Daphne Woodward. In a collection entitled A MAIGRET QUARTET. London: Hamish Hamilton, 1972. 416p. (Also includes MAIGRET'S FAILURE, MAIGRET IN SOCIETY and MAIGRET'S SPECIAL MURDER)

American Editions

________, tr. by Daphne Woodward. In a collection entitled A MAIGRET TRIO. New York: Harcourt Brace Jovanovich, 1973. 290p. (Also includes MAIGRET'S FAILURE and MAIGRET IN SOCIETY)

174. LE TRAIN. Paris: Presses de la Cité, 1961. 220p.

________. Paris: Presses de la Cité, 1965. 187p.

________. Paris: Presses de la Cité, 1970. 213p. (Collection "Simenon broché")

________. Paris: Presses de la Cité, 1972. 191p.

(Collection "Presses-Pocket," 914)

________. Paris: Presses de la Cité, 1973. 191p.

English Translations
British Editions

THE TRAIN, tr. by Robert Baldick. London: Hamish Hamilton, 1964. 142p.

________, tr. by Robert Baldick. Harmondsworth: Penguin Books, 1967. 141p. (paper)

American Editions

________, tr. by Robert Baldick. Bound with THE PREMIER, tr. by Daphne Woodward. New York: Harcourt Brace Jovanovich, 1966. 248p.

________, tr. by Robert Baldick. New York: Pocket Books, 1968. 155p. (paper)

1962

175. LES AUTRES. Paris: Presses de la Cité, 1962. 220p.

________. Appearing in La Revue de Paris, Nos. 5-7, 1962.

________. Paris: Presses de la Cité, 1966. 187p.

________. Paris: Presses de la Cité, 1970. 217p.

176. MAIGRET ET LE CLIENT DU SAMEDI. Paris: Presses de la Cité, 1962. 187p.

English Translations
British Editions

MAIGRET AND THE SATURDAY CALLER, tr. by Tony White. London: Hamish Hamilton, 1964. 128p.

________, tr. by Tony White. Harmondsworth: Penguin Books, 1964. 122p. (paper)

________, tr. by Tony White. Harmondsworth: Penguin Books, 1968. 123p. (paper)

177. MAIGRET ET LES BRAVES GENS. Paris: Presses de la Cité, 1962. 191p. (100 "de luxe" copies)

________, edited by Rene Daudon. New York: Harcourt, Brace & World, 1969. 230p. (paper) (student edition)

178. MAIGRET ET L'INSPECTEUR MALGRACIEUX. Paris: Presses de la Cité, 1962. 185p.

________. In a collection entitled TROIS NOUVELLES, edited by Frank W. Lindsay. Illustrated by Allyn Amundson. New York: Appleton-Century-Crofts, 1966. 228p. (Also includes LA PIPE DE MAIGRET and SOUS PEINE DE MORT)

________, edited by Geoffrey Goodall. London: Macmillan; New York: St. Martin's Press, 1969. viii, 69p. (paper) (Collection "Escrivac")

179. LA PORTE. Paris: Presses de la Cité, 1962. 216p.

________. Paris: Presses de la Cité, 1966. 187p. (Collection "Simenon broché")

________. Paris: Presses de la Cité, 1970. 222p.

<u>English Translations</u>

THE DOOR, tr. by Daphne Woodward. London: Hamish Hamilton, 1964. 140p.

________, tr. by Daphne Wood. Harmondsworth: Penguin Books, 1968. 138p. (paper)

<u>1963</u>

180. LES ANNEAUX DE BICETRE. Paris: Presses de la Cité, 1963. 318p. (100 numbered copies)

________. Paris: Presses de la Cité, 1966. 237p. (Collection "Simenon broché")

English Translations

THE PATIENT, tr. by Jean Stewart. London: Hamish Hamilton, 1963. viii, 236p.

________, tr. by Jean Stewart. Harmondsworth: Penguin Books, 1968. 206p. (paper)

American Editions

________, tr. by Jean Stewart. New York: Harcourt, Brace & World, 1964. 240p.

________, tr. by Jean Stewart. New York: New American Library, 1965. 192p. (paper)

181. LA COLERE DE MAIGRET. Paris: Presses de la Cité, 1963. (Collection "Maigret")

English Translations

MAIGRET LOSES HIS TEMPER, tr. by Robert Eglesfield. London: Hamish Hamilton, 1965. 140p.

________, tr. by Robert Eglesfield. Harmondsworth: Penguin Books, 1967. 139p. (paper)

________, tr. by Robert Eglesfield. London: White Lion, 1975. 140p.

American Editions

________, tr. by Robert Eglesfield. New York: Harcourt Brace Jovanovich, 1974. 138p. (Helen and Kurt Wolff Book)

182. ENTRETIEN AVEC ROGER STEPHANIE. Paris: Radio Télévision Française, 1963. 189p. (Interview done by Simenon on November 30 and December 7, 14 and 21, 1963.) (Nonfiction)

183. MA CONVICTION PROFONDE. Introduction by Roger Nordman. Geneva: Cailler, 1963. 125p. (Unedited writings of Georges Simenon)

184. MAIGRET ET LE CLOCHARD. Paris: Presses de la Cité, 1963. 189p. (100 numbered copies)

________, bound with LA PIPE DE MAIGRET. Paris: Editions G. P., 1966. 251p.

English Translations

MAIGRET AND THE DOSSIER, tr. by Jean Stewart. London: Hamish Hamilton, 1973. 155p.

American Editions

MAIGRET AND THE BUM, tr. by Jean Stewart. New York: Harcourt Brace Jovanovich, 1973. 149p.

185. LA PISTE DU HOLLANDAIS. In an untitled collection of short stories. Paris: Presses de la Cité, 1963. 181p. (Also includes LES DEMOISELLES DE QUEUE DE VACHE; LE MATIN DES TROIS ABSOUTES; LE NAUFRAGE DE "L'ARMOIRE A GLACE"; LES MAINS PLEINES; NICOLAS; and ANNETTE ET LA DAME BLONDE)

________. In Volume I of a collection entitled LES ENQUETES DU COMMISSAIRE MAIGRET. Paris: Presses de la Cité, 1966. 480p.

________. In an untitled collection of short stories. Paris: Presses de la Cité, 1973. 192p. (Same contents as the 1963 edition)

186. LA RUE AUX TROIS POUSSINS. Paris: Presses de la Cité, 1963. 315p. (50 numbered copies)

________. Paris: Presses de la Cité, 1967. 224p. (Collection "Simenon broché")

________. Paris: Presses de la Cité, 1972. 192p.

1964

187. LA CHAMBRE BLEUE. Paris: Presses de la Cité, 1964. 222p. (50 numbered copies) (Collection "Romans")

_______. Paris: Presses de la Cité, 1966. 187p. (Collection "Simenon broché")

_______. Paris: Presses de la Cité, 1972. 218p.

English Translations
British Editions

THE BLUE ROOM, tr. by Eileen Ellenbogen. London: Hamish Hamilton, 1965. 157p.

_______, tr. by Eileen Ellenbogen. Harmondsworth: Penguin Books, 1968. 150p. (paper)

American Editions

_______, tr. by Eileen Ellenbogen. Bound with THE ACCOMPLICES, tr. by Bernard Frechtman. New York: Harcourt, Brace & World, 1964. 284p.

_______, tr. by Eileen Ellenbogen. New York: New American Library, 1965. 127p. (paper)

188. L'HOMME AU PETIT CHIEN. Paris: Presses de la Cité, 1964. 251p. (Collection "Grands Romans")

_______. Paris: Presses de la Cité, 1966. 221p.

_______. Paris: Presses de la Cité, 1972. 242p.

English Translations
British Editions

THE MAN WITH THE LITTLE DOG, tr. by Jean Stewart. London: Hamish Hamilton, 1965. 159p.

189. MAIGRET ET LE FANTOME. Paris: Presses de la Cité, 1964. 187p. (Collection "Maigret")

________. Paris: Presses de la Cité, 1966. 186p.

________. Bound with MAIGRET HESITE. Illustrated by Jean Retailleau. Paris: Presses de la Cité, 1969. 356p.

190. MAIGRET SE DEFEND. Paris: Presses de la Cité, 1964. 185p. (60 "de luxe" copies constituting the original edition.)

English Translations
British Editions

MAIGRET ON THE DEFENSIVE, tr. by Alastair Hamilton. London: Hamish Hamilton, 1966. 143p.

________, tr. by Alastair Hamilton. Harmondsworth: Penguin Books, 128p. (paper)

________. In a collection entitled MAIGRET: A FIFTH OMNIBUS. London: Hamish Hamilton, 1973. 411p. (Also includes MADAME MAIGRET'S FRIEND, THE PATIENCE OF MAIGRET and MAIGRET TAKES THE WATERS)

1965

191. LA PATIENCE DE MAIGRET. Paris: Presses de la Cité, 1965. 187p. (50 numbered copies constituting the original edition.) (Collection "Maigret")

________. Paris: Presses de la Cité, 1970. 187p. (paper) (Collection "Presses-Pocket," 793)

English Translations
British Editions

THE PATIENCE OF MAIGRET, tr. by Alastair Hamilton. London: Hamish Hamilton, 1966.

________, tr. by Alistair Hamilton. In a collection entitled THE SECOND SIMENON OMNIBUS. Harmondsworth: Penguin Books, 1970. 382p. (paper) (Also includes THE ACCOMPLICES and MAIGRET'S PICKPOCKET)

________, tr. by Alastair Hamilton. In a collection entitled MAIGRET: A FIFTH OMNIBUS. London: Hamish Hamilton, 1973. 411p. (Also includes MADAME MAIGRET'S FRIEND, MAIGRET ON THE DEFENSIVE and MAIGRET TAKES THE WATERS)

192. LE PETIT SAINT. Presses de la Cité, 1965. 253p. (Collection "Romans")

________. Paris: Presses de la Cité, 1967. 192p. (Collection "Simenon broché")

________. Paris: Presses de la Cité, 1972. 244p.

English Translations
British Editions

THE LITTLE SAINT, tr. by Bernard Frechtman. London: Hamish Hamilton, 1966. 218p.

American Editions

________, tr. by Bernard Frechtman. New York: Harcourt, Brace & World, 1965. 186p.

________, tr. by Bernard Frechtman. New York: Pocket Books, 1967. 175p. (paper)

193. LE TRAIN DE VENISE. Paris: Presses de la Cité, 1965. 239p. (100 numbered copies constituting the original edition.)

________. Paris: Presses de la Cité, 1968. 192p. ("Nouvelle Collection brochée Simenon")

________. Paris: Presses de la Cité, 1972. 232p.

English Translations
British Editions

THE VENICE TRAIN, tr. by Alastair Hamilton. London: Hamish Hamilton, 1974. 152p.

American Editions

________, tr. by Alastair Hamilton. New York: Harcourt Brace Jovanovich, 1974. 143p. (Helen and and Kurt Wolff Book)

1966

194. LE CONFESSIONNAL. Paris: Presses de la Cité, 1966. 219p. (Collection "Romans")

________. Paris: Presses de la Cité, 1968. 192p. (Collection brochée "Simenon")

________. Paris: Presses de la Cité, 1971. 214p.

English Translations
British Editions

THE CONFESSIONAL, tr. by Jean Stewart. London: Hamish Hamilton, 1967. 155p.

________, tr. by Jean Stewart. In a collection entitled THE SEVENTH SIMENON OMNIBUS. Harmondsworth: Penguin Books, 1974. 395p. (paper) (Also includes MAIGRET AND THE KILLER and MAIGRET TAKES THE WATERS)

American Editions

________, tr. by Jean Stewart. New York: Harcourt Brace Jovanovich, 1968. 155p.

195. LES ENQUETES DU COMMISSAIRE MAIGRET. Volume I. Paris: Presses de la Cité, 1966. 480p. (Contents: LES MEMOIRES DE MAIGRET; SEPT PETITES CROIX DANS UN CARNET; LE PETIT RESTAURANT DE TERNES; LA PREMIERE ENQUETE DE MAIGRET; LE DUEL DE FONSINE; LE CRIME DU MALGRACIEUX; MON AMI MAIGRET; LA PISTE DU HOLLANDAIS.)

________. Volume II. Paris: Presses de la Cité, 1967. 472p. (Contents: MAIGRET AU "PICRATT'S"; LES VACANCES DE MAIGRET; MAI-

GRET ET L'HOMME DU BANC; MAIGRET ET LES PETITS COCHONS SANS QUEUES; UN CERTAIN M. BERQUIN; L'ESCALE DE BUENAVENTURA; MADAME QUATRE ET SES ENFANTS; LE DOCTEUR KIRKENS; LES DEMOISELLES DE QUEUE DE VACHE; LE NAUFRAGE DE "L'ARMOIRE A GLACE.")

196. LA MORT D'AUGUSTE. Paris: Presses de la Cité, 1966. 256p. (Collection "Romans")

________. Paris: Presses de la Cité, 1968. 192p. (Collection brochée "Simenon")

________. Paris: Presses de la Cité, 1971. 252p.

English Translations
British Editions

THE OLD MAN DIES, tr. by Bernard Frechtman. London: Hamish Hamilton, 1968. 152p.

________, tr. by Bernard Frechtman. In a collection entitled THE THIRD MAIGRET OMNIBUS. Harmondsworth: Penguin Books, 1971. 366p. (paper) (Also includes MAIGRET HAS DOUBTS and MAIGRET AND THE MINISTER.)

American Editions

________, tr. by Bernard Frechtman. New York: Harcourt, Brace & World, 1967. 152p.

197. MAIGRET ET L'AFFAIRE NAHOUR. Paris: Presses de la Cité, 1966. 192p. (65 "de luxe" copies)

________. Paris: Presses de la Cité, 1967. 188p. (Collection "Maigret")

________. Paris: Presses de la Cité, 1969. 187p.

________. Paris: Presses de la Cité, 1971. 187p. (paper) (Collection "Presses-Pocket," 832)

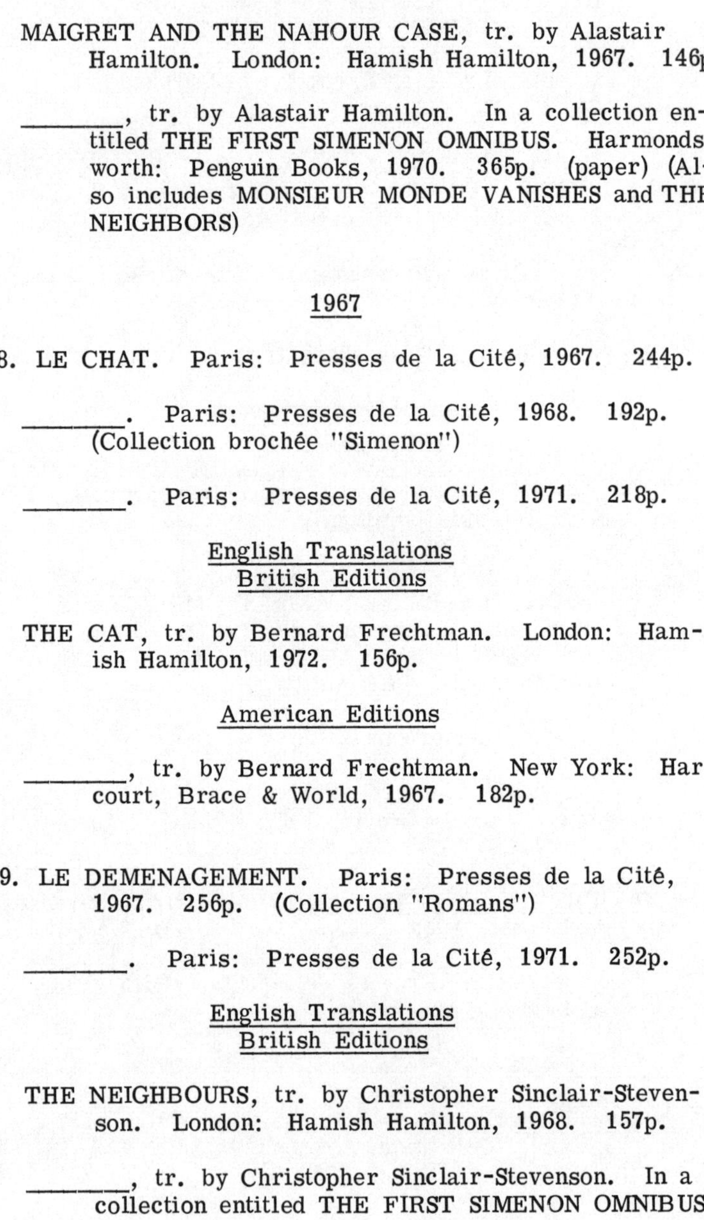

English Translations
British Editions

MAIGRET AND THE NAHOUR CASE, tr. by Alastair Hamilton. London: Hamish Hamilton, 1967. 146p.

________, tr. by Alastair Hamilton. In a collection entitled THE FIRST SIMENON OMNIBUS. Harmondsworth: Penguin Books, 1970. 365p. (paper) (Also includes MONSIEUR MONDE VANISHES and THE NEIGHBORS)

1967

198. LE CHAT. Paris: Presses de la Cité, 1967. 244p.

________. Paris: Presses de la Cité, 1968. 192p. (Collection brochée "Simenon")

________. Paris: Presses de la Cité, 1971. 218p.

English Translations
British Editions

THE CAT, tr. by Bernard Frechtman. London: Hamish Hamilton, 1972. 156p.

American Editions

________, tr. by Bernard Frechtman. New York: Harcourt, Brace & World, 1967. 182p.

199. LE DEMENAGEMENT. Paris: Presses de la Cité, 1967. 256p. (Collection "Romans")

________. Paris: Presses de la Cité, 1971. 252p.

English Translations
British Editions

THE NEIGHBOURS, tr. by Christopher Sinclair-Stevenson. London: Hamish Hamilton, 1968. 157p.

________, tr. by Christopher Sinclair-Stevenson. In a collection entitled THE FIRST SIMENON OMNIBUS.

Harmondsworth: Penguin Books, 1970. 365p. (paper) (Also includes MONSIEUR MONDE VANISHES and MAIGRET AND THE NAHOUR CASE)

American Editions

THE MOVE, tr. by Christopher Sinclair-Stevenson. New York: Harcourt, Brace & World, 1968. 148p.

200. OEUVRES COMPLETES. (Novels and Short Stories.) Collection established by Gilbert Sigaux. Volumes I-III. Lausanne: Editions Rencontre, 1967. 608p., 568p., 567p.

________. Volumes IV-XV. Lausanne: Editions Rencontre, 1967-1968. 567p., 592p., 512p., 439p., 480p., 576p., 568p., 496p., 615p., 576p.

________. Volumes XVI-XXVI. Lausanne: Editions Rencontre, 1968? 477p., 335p., 336p., 327p., 464p., 472p., 480p., 584p., 607p., 461p., 429p.

________. Volumes XXVII-XXXVI. Lausanne: Editions Rencontre, 1969? 528p., 511p., 501p., 509p., 507p., 487p., 507p., 459p., 519p., 464p.

________. Volumes XXXVII-XLI. Lausanne: Editions Rencontre, 1970. 416p., 559p., 485p., 461p., 491p.

201. OEUVRES COMPLETES MAIGRET. Collection established by Gilbert Sigaux. Volumes I-III. Lausanne: Editions Rencontre, 1967. 539p., 549p., 362p.

________. Volumes IV-XV. Lausanne: Editions Rencontre, 1968? 527p., 552p., 566p., 539p., 607p., 568p., 447p., 552p., 543p., 487p., 584p.

________. Volumes XVI-XXIV. Lausanne: Editions Rencontre, 1969? 639p., 487p., 461p., 456p., 565p., 551p., 567p., 477p.

________. Volume XXV. Lausanne: Editions Rencontre, 1970? 413p.

202. LE VOLEUR DE MAIGRET. Paris: Presses de la Cité, 1967. 192p. (Collection "Maigret")

________. Paris: Presses de la Cité, 1971. 182p. (paper)

English Translations
British Editions

MAIGRET'S PICKPOCKET, tr. by Nigel Ryan. London: Hamish Hamilton, 1968. 151p.

________, tr. by Nigel Ryan. In a collection entitled THE SECOND SIMENON OMNIBUS. Harmondsworth: Penguin Books, 1970. 382p. (paper) (Also includes THE PATIENCE OF MAIGRET and THE ACCOMPLICES)

American Editions

________, tr. by Nigel Ryan. New York: Harcourt Brace Jovanovich, 1968. 151p.

1968

203. L'AMI D'ENFANCE DE MAIGRET. Paris: Presses de la Cité, 1968. 251p. (Collection "Romans")

________. Paris: Presses de la Cité, 1969. 192p. (Collection "Maigret")

English Translations
British Editions

MAIGRET'S BOYHOOD FRIEND, tr. by Eileen Ellenbogen. London: Hamish Hamilton, 1970. 189p.

________, tr. by Eileen Ellenbogen. In a collection entitled A FIFTH SIMENON OMNIBUS. Harmondsworth: Penguin Books, 1972. 400p. (paper) (Also includes BIG BOB and NOVEMBER)

American Editions

________, tr. by Eileen Ellenbogen. New York: Harcourt Brace Jovanovich, 1970. 182p.

204\. MAIGRET A VICHY. Paris: Presses de la Cité, 1968. 254p.

________. Paris: Presses de la Cité, 1968. 192p. (Collection "Maigret")

English Translations
British Editions

MAIGRET TAKES THE WATERS, tr. by Eileen Ellenbogen. London: Hamish Hamilton, 1969. 176p.

________, tr. by Eileen Ellenbogen. In a collection entitled MAIGRET: A FIFTH OMNIBUS. London: Hamish Hamilton, 1973. 411p. (Also includes MADAME MAIGRET'S FRIEND, MAIGRET ON THE DEFENSIVE and THE PATIENCE OF MAIGRET)

________, tr. by Eileen Ellenbogen. In a collection entitled THE SEVENTH SIMENON OMNIBUS. Harmondsworth: Penguin Books, 1974. 395p. (paper) (Also includes MAIGRET AND THE KILLER and THE CONFESSIONAL)

American Editions

MAIGRET IN VICHY, tr. by Eileen Ellenbogen. New York: Harcourt Brace Jovanovich, 1969. 177p.

________, tr. by Eileen Ellenbogen. New York: Avon, 1970. 192p. (paper)

205\. MAIGRET HESITE. Paris: Presses de la Cité, 1968. 258p. (Collection "Romans")

________. Paris: Presses de la Cité, 1969. 192p. (Collection "Maigret")

________ bound with MAIGRET ET LA FANTOME. Paris: Presses de la Cité, 1969. 356p.

English Translations
British Editions

MAIGRET HESITATES, tr. by Lyn Moir. London: Hamish Hamilton, 1970. 175p.

American Editions

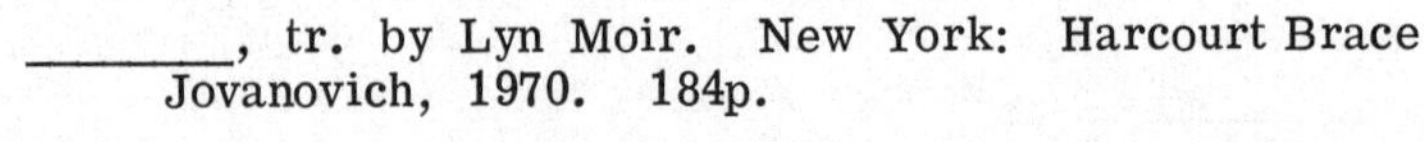

________, tr. by Lyn Moir. New York: Harcourt Brace Jovanovich, 1970. 184p.

206. LA MAIN. Paris: Presses de la Cité, 1968. 246p.

________. Paris: Presses de la Cité, 1971. 246p.

English Translations
British Editions

THE MAN ON THE BENCH IN THE BARN, tr. by Moura Budberg. London: Hamish Hamilton, 1970. 170p.

American Editions

________, tr. by Moura Budberg. New York: Harcourt Brace Jovanovich, 1970. 188p.

207. LA PRISON. Paris: Presses de la Cité, 1968. 256p. (Collection "Romans")

________. Paris: Presses de la Cité, 1971. 256p.

English Translations
British Editions

THE PRISON, tr. by Lyn Moir. London: Hamish Hamilton, 1969. 191p.

________, tr. by Lyn Moir. In a collection entitled THE SIXTH SIMENON OMNIBUS. Harmondsworth: Penguin Books, 1973. 462p. (paper) (Also includes MAIGRET AND THE WINE MERCHANT and THE RICH MAN)

American Editions

________, tr. by Lyn Moir. New York: Harcourt Brace Jovanovich, 1969. 182p.

1969

208. IL Y A ENCORE DES NOISETIERS. Paris: Presses de la Cité, 1969. 254p. (Collection "Romans")

________. Paris: Presses de la Cité, 1972. 246p.

209. MAIGRET ET LE TUEUR. Paris: Presses de la Cité, 1969. 258p. (Collection "Romans")

________. Paris: Presses de la Cité, 1971. 190p.

LE MEURTRE D'UN ETUDIANT, edited by Frédéric Ernst. New York: Holt, 1971. ix, 171p. (paper) (Published in France as MAIGRET ET LE TUEUR.)

English Translations
British Editions

MAIGRET AND THE KILLER, tr. by Lyn Moir. London: Hamish Hamilton, 1971. 155p.

________, tr. by Lyn Moir. In a collection entitled THE SEVENTH SIMENON OMNIBUS. Harmondsworth: Penguin Books, 1974. 395p. (paper) (Also includes THE CONFESSIONAL and MAIGRET TAKES THE WATERS)

American Editions

________, tr. by Lyn Moir. New York: Harcourt Brace Jovanovich, 1971. 165p.

210. NOVEMBRE. Paris: Presses de la Cité, 1969. 258p. (Collection "Romans")

________. Paris: Presses de la Cité, 1972. 219p.

English Translations
British Editions

NOVEMBER, tr. by Jean Stewart. London: Hamish Hamilton, 1970. 155p.

________, tr. by Jean Stewart. In a collection entitled

A FIFTH SIMENON OMNIBUS. Harmondsworth: Penguin Books, 1972. 400p. (paper) (Also includes MAIGRET'S BOYHOOD FRIEND and BIG BOB)

American Edition

________, tr. by Jean Stewart. New York: Harcourt Brace Jovanovich, 1970. 185p.

211. LE PARIS DE SIMENON. Illustrated by Frédérick Franck. Paris: Tehou, 1969. 191p. (Nonfiction)

________. Illustrated by Frédérick Franck. Brussels: Dessart-Tolra, 1969. 191p.

English Translations
British Editions

SIMENON'S PARIS. Illustrated by Frederick Franck. London: Ebury Press, 1970. 192p.

American Edition

________. Illustrated by Frederick Franck. New York: Dial Press, 1970. 191p.

Titles First Published in the 1970s

1970

212. LA FOLLE DE MAIGRET. Paris: Presses de la Cité. 1970. 254p. (Collection "Romans")

_______. Paris: Presses de la Cité, 1972. 186p.

English Translations
British Editions

MAIGRET AND THE MADWOMAN, tr. by Eileen Ellenbogen. London: Hamish Hamilton, 1972. 184p.

American Editions

_______, tr. by Eileen Ellenbogen. New York: Harcourt Brace Jovanovich, 1972. 176p. (Helen and Kurt Wolff Book)

213. MAIGRET ET LE MARCHAND DE VIN. Paris: Presses de la Cité, 1970. 248p.

_______. Paris: Presses de la Cité, 1971. 186p.

English Translations
British Editions

MAIGRET AND THE WINE MERCHANT, tr. by Eileen Ellenbogen. London: Hamish Hamilton, 1971. 172p.

_______, tr. by Eileen Ellenbogen. In a collection entitled THE SIXTH SIMENON OMNIBUS. Harmondsworth: Penguin Books, 1973. 426p. (Also includes THE PRISON and THE RICH MAN)

American Editions

________, tr. by Eileen Ellenbogen. New York: Harcourt Brace Jovanovich, 1971. 187p.

________, tr. by Eileen Ellenbogen. New York: Curtis Books, 1972. 160p. (paper)

214. QUAND J'ETAIS VIEUX. Paris: Presses de la Cité, 1970. 407p. (Collection "Romans")

________. Volumes I-III. Paris: Presses de la Cité, 1972. 3 vols. 181p., 182p., 185p.

English Translations
British Editions

WHEN I WAS OLD, tr. by Helen Eustis. London: Hamish Hamilton, 1972. 343p.

________, tr. by Helen Eustis. Harmondsworth: Penguin Books, 1972. 332p. (paper)

American Editions

________, tr. by Helen Eustis. New York: Harcourt Brace Jovanovich, 1971. 343p.

215. LE RICHE HOMME. Paris: Presses de la Cité, 1970. 280p. (Collection "Romans")

________. Paris: Presses de la Cité, 1970. 246p.

________. Paris: Presses de la Cité, 1973. 189p.

English Translations
British Editions

THE RICH MAN, tr. by Jean Stewart. London: Hamish Hamilton, 1971. 150p.

________, tr. by Jean Stewart. In a collection entitled THE SIXTH SIMENON OMNIBUS. Harmondsworth: Penguin Books, 1973. 426p. (paper) (Also includes MAIGRET AND THE WINE MERCHANT and THE RICH MAN)

American Editions

_______, tr. by Jean Stewart. New York: Harcourt Brace Jovanovich, 1971. 183p.

1971

216. LE CAGE DE VERRE. Paris: Presses de la Cité, 1971. 242p.

_______. Paris: Club Français du Livre, 1971. 247p. (Collection "Le Grand Livre du Mois")

_______. Paris: Presses de la Cité, 1973. 185p.

English Translations
British Editions

THE GLASS CAGE, tr. by Antonia White. London: Hamish Hamilton, 1973. 156p.

American Editions

_______, tr. by Antonia White. New York: Harcourt Brace Jovanovich, 1973. 148p. (A Helen and Kurt Wolff Book)

217. LA DISPARITION D'ODILE. Paris: Club Française du Livre, 1971. 255p. (Collection "Le Grand Livre du Mois")

_______. Paris: Presses de la Cité, 1971. 253p.

_______. Paris: Presses de la Cité, 1973. 187p.

English Translations
British Editions

THE DISAPPEARANCE OF ODILE, tr. by Lyn Moir. London: Hamish Hamilton, 1972. 156p.

American Editions

_______, tr. by Lyn Moir. New York: Harcourt Brace Jovanovich, 1972. 183p. (A Helen and Kurt Wolff Book)

218. MAIGRET ET L'HOMME TOUT SEUL. Paris: Presses de la Cité, 1971. 251p.

________. Paris: Presses de la Cité, 1972. 185p.

English Translations
British Editions

MAIGRET AND THE LONER, tr. by Eileen Ellenbogen. London: Hamish Hamilton, 1975. 187p.

219. MAIGRET ET L'INDICATEUR. Paris: Presses de la Cité, 1971. 248p.

________. Paris: Presses de la Cité, 1973. 189p.

English Translations
British Editions

MAIGRET AND THE FLEA, tr. by Lyn Moir. London: Hamish Hamilton, 1972. 150p.

American Editions

MAIGRET AND THE INFORMER, tr. by Lyn Moir. New York: Harcourt Brace Jovanovich, 1972. 150p. (A Helen and Kurt Wolff Book)

1972

220. CHOIX DE SIMENON, edited by Frank W. Lindsay and Anthony M. Nazzaro. New York: Appleton-Century-Crofts, 1972, vii, 213p. (short stories). (Contents: L'ETRANGLEUR DE MORET; LE DUEL DE FONSINE; LE CRIME DU MALGRACIEUX; LES MAINS PLEINES; LES TROIS REMBRANDT; LES DEMOISELLES DE QUEUE DE VACHE; LA VIEILLE DAME DE BAYEUX)

221. LES INNOCENTS. Paris: Presses de la Cité, 1972. 183p.

________. Paris: Presses de la Cité, 1973. 185p.

English Translations
British Editions

THE INNOCENTS, tr. by Eileen Ellenbogen. London: Hamish Hamilton, 1973. 188p.

American Editions

_______, tr. by Eileen Ellenbogen. New York: Harcourt Brace Jovanovich, 1973. 160p. (A Helen and Kurt Wolff Book)

222. MAIGRET ET MONSIEUR CHARLES. Paris: Presses de la Cité, 1972. 194p.

_______. Paris: Presses de la Cité, 1973. 187p. (Collection "Maigret")

English Translations
British Editions

MAIGRET AND MONSIEUR CHARLES, tr. by Marianne A. Sinclair. London: Hamish Hamilton, 1973. 156p.

APPENDIX

Sources for Part III

American Book Publishing Record. New York: Bowker, 1960- . v. 1- .

Biblio: Catalogue des Ouvrages Parus en Langue Française dans le Monde Entier. Paris: Hachette, 1933- .

Bibliographical Index; A Cumulative Bibliography of Bibliographies, 1938- . New York: H. W. Wilson, 1938- .

Bibliographie de la France: Livres d'Etrennes, 1974. Paris: Cercle de la Librairie, 1974.

_______; Livres d'Etrennes, 1975. Paris: Cercle de La Librairie, 1975.

British Museum. Department of Printed Books. General Catalogue of Printed Books. London: Clowes, 1931-1966. 263v.

_______. Ten-Year Supplement, 1956-1965. London: Trustees of the British Museum, 1968. 50v.

_______. Five-Year Supplement, 1966-1970. London: Trustees of the British Museum, 1971-1972. 26v.

British National Bibliography. London: Council of the British National Bibliography, 1950- .

Cumulative Book Index, A World's List of Books in the English Language. New York: H. W. Wilson, 1898- .

The English Catalogue of Books, 1801- . London: Publishers' Circular, 1864- .

de Fallois, Bernard. Simenon. Paris: Gallimard, 1961.

Hagen, Ordean A. Who Done It? A Guide to Detective Mystery and Suspense Fiction. New York: Bowker, 1969.

La Librairie Française; Catalogue Général des Ouvrages Parus du 1er Janvier 1946 au 1er Janvier 1956. Paris: Cercle de la Librairie, 1957. 4v.

_______; Catalogue Général des Ouvrages Parus du 1er Janvier 1956 au 1er Janvier 1966. Paris: Cercle de la Librairie, 1968. 4v.

_______; Les Livres de L'Année, 1966-1970. Paris: Cercle de la Librairie, 1967-1971. 5v.

Narcejac, Thomas. The Art of Simenon. Translated by Cynthia Rowland. London: Routledge & Kegan Paul, 1952.

Paris: Bibliothèque Nationale. Catalogue Général des Livres Imprimés de la Bibliothèque Nationale. Paris: Imprimerie Nationale, 1897- . v. 1- .

_______. Catalogue Général des Livres Imprimés de la Bibliothèque Nationale, 1960-1964. Paris: Imprimerie Nationale, 1965-1967. 12v.

Raymond, John. Simenon in Court. London: Hamish Hamilton, 1968.

U.S. Library of Congress. A Catalog of Books Represented by Library of Congress Printed Cards Issued to July 31, 1942. Ann Arbor: Edwards, 1942-1946. 167v.

_______. Supplement, 1942-1947. Ann Arbor: Edwards, 1948. 42v.

_______. Author Catalog; A Cumulative List of Works Represented by Library of Congress Printed Cards, 1948-1952. Ann Arbor: Edwards, 1953. 23v.

_______. The National Union Catalog; A Cumulative Author List Representing Library of Congress Printed Cards, 1953-1957. Ann Arbor: Edwards, 1958. 28v.

_______. The National Union Catalog, 1958-1962. New

York: Rowman and Littlefield, 1963. 54v.

________. The National Union Catalog, 1963-1967. Washington, D.C.: Library of Congress, 1969. 67v.

________. The National Union Catalog, 1968-1972. Washington, D.C.: Library of Congress, 1973. 104v.

________. The National Union Catalog, 1973- . Washington, D.C.: Library of Congress, 1974- .

________. The National Union Catalog, 1952 to 1955 Imprints. Ann Arbor: Edwards, 1961. 30v.

University of California. Institute of Library Research. Union Catalog of Monographs Cataloged by the Nine Campuses. From 1963-1967; Author Titles. Berkeley: University of California, 1972. 31v.

University of California. Berkeley Library. Author-Title Catalog. Boston, G. K. Hall, 1963. 115v.

University of California. Los Angeles. Dictionary Catalog of the University Library, 1919-1962. Boston: G. K. Hall, 1963. 192v.

INDEX TO FRENCH TITLES

(Numbers refer to the entry number)

A L'Ombre de Saint Nicolas 102
L'Affaire Saint Fiacre 12
L'Aîné des Ferchaux 79
L'Ami d'enfance de Maigret 203
L'Amie de Mme Maigret 111
L'Âne rouge 23
Les Anneaux de Bicêtre 180
Annette et la dame blonde 185
Antoine et Julie 133
L'Assassin 41
Au bout du rouleau 86
Au rendez-vous des terre-neuvas 1
Les Autres 175

Le Baron de l'Ecluse 139
Le Bateau d'Emile 139
Bergelon 63
Betty 172
Le Bilan Malétras 97
Le Blanc à lunettes 42
La Boule noire 147
Le Bourgmestre de Furnes 58

Le Cage de verre 216
Les Caves du Majestic 70
Cécile est morte 70
Le Cercle des Mahé 83
Un Certain M. Berquin 195
Ceux de la soif 45
Le Châle de Marie Doudon 44, 66
La Chambre bleue 187
le Charretier de la "Providence" 2
le Chat 198
Chemin sans issue 46
le Cheval blanc 47

Chez Krull 59
Chez les Flamands 13
Le Chien jaune 3
Choix de Simenon 220
le Clan des Ostendais 87
le Client le plus obstiné du monde 88
Les Clients d'Avrenos 34
la Colère de Maigret 181
le Commissaire Maigret et L'Inspecteur Malchanceux 88, 89, 93, 96
les Complices 148
le Confessionnal 194
Une Confidence de Maigret 162
le Coup de lune 24
le Coup de vague 60
Cour d'assises 64
Le Crime du Malgracieux 195, 220
Un Crime en Hollande 4
Crime impuni 140
La Croisière du "Potam" 139

La Danseuse du Gai-Moulin 5
Le Déménagement 199
Le Demoiselles de Concarneau 37
Les Demoiselles de queue de vache 185, 195, 220
Le Destin des Malou 98
Dimanche 163
La Disparition d'Odile 217
Le Docteur Kirkens 195
Le Doigt de Barraquier 139
Les Dossiers de l'agence O 74
Le Duel de Fonsine 139, 195, 220

Un Echec de Maigret 151
L'Ecluse no. 1 25
En cas de malheur 152
L'Enigme de la "Marie-Galante" 53
Les Enquêtes du Commissaire Maigret 103, 108, 114, 117, 121, 124, 137, 185, 195
L'Enterrement de Monsieur Bouvet 112
L'Etrangleur de Moret 220
Entretien avec Roger Stéphanie 182
L'Epingle en fer à cheval 139
L'Escale de Buenaventura 114, 195
L'Escalier de fer 134
L'Evadé 38

Les Fantômes du Chapelier 104
Faubourg 43
Félicie est là 78
La Femme du pilote 139
La Femme en France 166
La Fenêtre des Rouet 80
Feux rouges 135
Les Fiançailles de Mr. Hire 26
Le Fils 153
Le Fils Cardinaud 69
La Folle de Maigret 212
Le Fond de la Bouteille 105
Le Fou de Bergerac 14
Les Frères Rico 128
La Fuite du Monsieur Monde 81

G7 53
Les Gens d'en face 27
Le Grand Bob 141
Le Grand Langoustier 53
La Guinguette à deux sous 15

Le Haut-Mal 28
L'Homme à barbe 139
L'Homme au petit chien 188
L'Homme de la Tour Eiffel (see La Tête d'un homme) 11
L'Homme de Londres 30
L'Homme qui regardait passer les trains 48
L'Horloger d'Everton 142

Il pleut, bergère... 65
Il y a encore des noisetiers 208
L'Inspecteur Cadavre 78
Les Inconnus dans la maison 61
Les Innocents 221

Je me souviens 82
La Jument perdue 99

Lettre à mon juge 90
"Liberty Bar" 16
Le Locataire 31
Long cours 39
Long cours sur les rivières et canaux 129

M. Gallet décédé 6
Ma conviction profonde 183

Madame Quatre et ses enfants 195
Maigret 32
Maigret à l'école 143
Maigret à New York 91
Maigret a peur 136
Maigret à Vichy 204
Maigret au "Picratts" 117
Maigret aux assises 167
Maigret chez le coroner 106
Maigret chez le ministre 144
Maigret en meublé 118
Maigret et la grande perche 119
Maigret et la jeune morte 145
Maigret et la vieille dame 107
Maigret et l'affaire Nahour 197
Maigret et le client du samedi 176
Maigret et le clochard 184
Maigret et le corps sans tête 149
Maigret et le fantôme 189
Maigret et le marchand de vin 213
Maigret et le tueur 209
Maigret et le voleur paresseux 173
Maigret et les braves gens 177
Maigret et les petits cochons sans queues 114
Maigret et les témoins récalcitrants 164
Maigret et les vieillards 168
Maigret et l'homme du blanc 137
Maigret et l'homme tout seul 218
Maigret et l'indicateur 219
Maigret et l'inspecteur Malgracieux 178
Maigret et Monsieur Charles 222
Maigret et son mort 100
Maigret hésite 205
Maigret, Lognon et les gangsters 130
Maigret revient 70
Maigret s'amuse 154
Maigret se défend 190
Maigret se fâche 92
Maigret se trompe 138
Maigret tend un piège 150
Maigret voyage 157
La Main 206
Les Mains pleines 185, 220
La Maison des sept jeunes filles 66
La Maison du canal 29
La Maison du juge 70
La Maison envahie 102

Malempin 62
La Marie du port 49
Marie qui louche 120
Le Matin des trois absoutes 185
La Mauvaise étoile 50
Les Mémoires de Maigret 121
Le Meurtre d'un étudiant 209
Mon ami Maigret 108
Monsieur La Souris 51
La Mort d'Auguste 196
La Mort de Belle 131

Le Naufrage de "L'Armoire à Glace" 185, 195
Le Nègre 155
Le Nègre s'est endormi 139
La Neige était sale 101
Nicolas 114, 185
Les Noces de Poitiers 84
Un Noel de Maigret 122
Un Nouveau dans la ville 113
Les Nouvelles enquêtes de Maigret 76
Nouvelles exotiques 78
Novembre 210
La Nuit des sept minutes 53
La Nuit du carrefour 7

Oeuvres complètes 200
Oeuvres complètes Maigret 201
L'Ombre chinoise 17
Omnibus Simenon 123
On ne tue pas les pauvres types 93
Oncle Charles s'est enfermé 71
L'Ours en peluche 169
L'Outlaw 67

Le Paris de Simenon 211
Le Passage de la ligne 158
Le Passager clandestin 94
Le Passager du "Polarlys" 18
La Patience de Maigret 191
Pedigree 102
Le Pendu de Saint-Pholien 8
Le Petit docteur 75
Le Petit homme d'Arkhangelsk 156
Le Petit restaurant de Ternes 122, 195
Le Petit Saint 192
Les Petits cochons sans queues 114

Pietr-Le-Letton 9
La Pipe de Maigret 95
La Piste du Hollandais 185
Les Pitard 35
Le Port des brumes 19
La Porte 179
La Première enquête de Maigret, 1913 109
Le Président 159
La Prison 207

Quand j'étais vieux 214
Quand les lampes sont éteintes 102
Quartier nègre 36
45° à L'ombre 40
Les Quatre jours du pauvre homme 110

Le Rapport du gendarme 77
Le Relais d'Alsace 10
Les Rescapés du "Télémaque" 52
Le Revolver de Maigret 132
Le Riche homme 215
Le Roman de L'homme 170
La Rue aux trois poussins 186

Les Scrupules de Maigret 160
Les Sept minutes (or G_7) 53
Sept petites croix dans un carnet 124
Signé Picpus 78
Les Soeurs LaCroix 54
Sous peine de mort 95
Strip-tease 161
Les Suicidés 33
Le Suspect 55

Tante Jeanne 115
Le Témoignage de l'enfant de choeur 96
Les Témoins 146
Le Temps d'Anaïs 125
Le Testament Donadieu 44
La Tête d'un homme 11
Touriste de bananes 56
Tournants dangereux 96, 114
Le Train 174
Le Train de Venise 193
Les Treize coupables 20
Les Treize énigmes 21
Les Treize mystères 22

Trois chambres à Manhattan 85
Les Trois crimes de mes amis 57
Trois nouvelles 95, 178
Les Trois Rembrandt 220

Les Vacances de Maigret 103
Valerie s'en va 139
La Vérité sur bébé Donge 72
Le Veuf 171
La Veuve Couderc 73
Une Vie comme neuve 126
Le Vieillard au porte-mine 127
La Vieille 165
La Vieille dame de Bayeux 220
Les Volets verts 116
Le Voleur de Maigret 202
Le Voyageur de la Toussaint 68

INDEX TO ENGLISH TRANSLATIONS

The Accomplices 148
Account Unsettled 140
Across the Street 80
Act of Passion 90
Affairs of Destiny 28, 30
An American Omnibus 128, 131, 135, 142
At the "Gai-Moulin" 5
Aunt Jeanne 115

Banana Tourist 56
A Battle of Nerves 11
Belle 131
The Bells of Bicêtre 180
Betty 172
Big Bob 141
Black Rain 65
Blind Alley 46
Blind Path 46
The Blue Room 187
The Bottom of the Bottle 105
Breton Sisters 37
The Brothers Rico 128
The Burgomaster of Furnes 58
The Burial of Monsieur Bouvet 112

The Cat 198
Chez Krull 59
A Chit of a Girl 49
The Confessional 194
The Crime at Lock 14 2
A Crime in Holland 4
The Crime of Inspector Maigret 8
The Crossroad Murders 7

Danger Ahead 135, 142
Danger Ashore 27
Danger at Sea 18

Death of a Harbour (Harbor) Master 19
The Death of M. Gallet 6
Destinations 112, 135
Disappearance of Odile 27
Disintegration of J. P. G. 38
The Door 179

Escape in Vain 31, 33

Face for a Clue 3
The Fate of the Malous 98
A Fifth Simenon Omnibus 141, 203, 210
First Born 79
The First Simenon Omnibus 81, 197, 199
Five Times Maigret 117, 138, 143, 160, 164
The Flemish Shop 13
Four Days in a Lifetime 110
Fugitive 140

The Gendarme's Report 77
The Girl in His Past 125
The Girl in Waiting 49
The Glass Cage 216
The Green Thermos 54
Guinguette by the Seine 15

The Hatter's Ghosts 104
Havoc by Accident 37, 42
The Heart of a Man 116
The Hitchhiker 135
Home Town 43
The House by the Canal 29

I Take This Woman 72
In Case of Emergency 152
In Two Latitudes 18, 24
The Innocents 221
Inquest on Bouvet 112
Inspector Maigret and the Burglar's Wife 119
Inspector Maigret and the Dead Girl 145
Inspector Maigret and the Killers 130
Inspector Maigret and the Strangled Stripper 117
Inspector Maigret in New York's Underworld 91
Inspector Maigret Investigates 7, 9
Introducing Inspector Maigret 6, 8
The Iron Staircase 134

Journey Backward into Time 122
The Judge and the Hatter 104, 146
Justice 64

Liberty Bar 16
Little Man from Archangel 156
The Little Saint 192
Lock at Charenton 25
The Lodger 31
Lost Moorings 46, 56

Madame Maigret's Friend 111
Madame Maigret's Own Case 111
The Madman of Bergerac 14
The Magician 133
Magnet of Doom 79
Maigret: A Fifth Omnibus 111, 190, 191, 204
Maigret Abroad 4, 5
Maigret Afraid 136
Maigret and M. L'Abbe 10, 19
Maigret and the Bum 184
Maigret and the Burglar's Wife 119
Maigret and the Calame Report 144
Maigret and the Dossier 184
Maigret and the Enigmatic Lett 9
Maigret and the Flea 219
Maigret and the Gangsters 130
Maigret and the Headless Corpse 149
Maigret and the Hundred Gibbets 8
Maigret and the Informer 219
Maigret and the Killer 209
Maigret and the Lazy Burglar 173
Maigret and the Loner 217
Maigret and the Madwoman 212
Maigret and the Millionaires 157
Maigret and the Minister 144
Maigret and Monsieur Charles 222
Maigret and the Nahour Case 197
Maigret and the Old Lady 107
Maigret and the Reluctant Witnesses 164
Maigret and the Saturday Caller 176
Maigret and the Young Girl 145
Maigret and the Wine Merchant 213
Maigret at the Crossroads 7
Maigret Cinq 107, 109, 118, 145, 154
Maigret Goes Home 12
Maigret Goes to School 143

Maigret Has Doubts 162
Maigret Has Scruples 160
Maigret Hesitates 205
Maigret in Court 167
Maigret in Montmartre 117
Maigret in New York 91
Maigret in Society 168
Maigret in New York's Underworld 91
Maigret in Vichy 204
Maigret Keeps a Rendezvous 1, 12
Maigret Loses His Temper 181
Maigret Meets a Milord 2
Maigret Mystified 17
A Maigret Omnibus 117, 138, 143, 160, 164
Maigret on Holiday 103
Maigret on the Defensive 190
A Maigret Quartet 100, 151, 168, 178
Maigret Rents a Room 118
Maigret Returns 32
Maigret Right and Wrong 117, 138
Maigret Sets a trap 150
Maigret Sits It Out 25, 32
Maigret Stonewalled 6
Maigret Takes a Room 118
Maigret Takes the Waters 204
Maigret to the Rescue 13, 15
Maigret Travels South 14, 16
Maigret Trio 151, 168, 173
Maigret Triumphant 108, 119, 132, 136, 167
Maigret's Boyhood Friend 203
Maigret's Christmas 122
Maigret's Dead Man 100
Maigret's Failure 151
Maigret's First Case 109
Maigret's Little Joke 154
Maigret's Memoirs 121
Maigret's Mistake 138
Maigret's Pickpocket 202
Maigret's Revolver 132
Maigret's Special Murder 100
The Man from Everywhere 10
The Man on the Bench in the Barn 206
The Man Who Watched the Trains Go By 48
The Man with the Dog 188
The Methods of Maigret 108
Mr. Hire's Engagement 26
Monsieur La Souris 51

Monsieur Monde Vanishes 81
The Most Obstinate Man in Paris 88
The Mouse 51
The Move 199
The Murderer 41
My Friend Maigret 108
The Mystery of the "Polarlys" 18

Negro 155
The Neighbours 199
A New Lease of Life 126
A New Lease on Life 126
Newhaven-Dieppe 30
No Vacation for Maigret 103
None of Maigret's Business 154
The Novel of a Man 170
November 210

The Old Lady of Bayeux 122
The Old Man Dies 196
On Land and Sea 18, 27
On the Danger Line 43, 55
One Way Out 33
The Ostenders 87

The Patience of Maigret (translation of Le Chien jaune and La Tête d'un homme) 3, 11
The Patience of Maigret (translation of La Patience de Maigret) 191
The Patient 180
Pedigree 102
Poisoned Relations 54
The Premier 159
The Prison 207

Red Lights 135
The Rich Man 215

Sacrifice 26, 69
The Sailor's Rendezvous 1
The Saint Fiacre Affair 12
Satan's Children 72, 110
The Second Maigret Omnibus 107, 109, 118, 145, 154
The Second Simenon Omnibus (Hamish Hamilton) 59, 116, 161, 171
The Second Simenon Omnibus (Penguin Books) 148, 191, 202
A Sense of Guilt 59, 116

The Seventh Simenon Omnibus 194, 204, 209
The Shadow Falls 44
The Shadow in the Courtyard 17
The Short Cases of Inspector Maigret 88, 122
A Simenon Omnibus 26, 152, 156, 159, 163
Simenon's Paris 211
The Sixth Simenon Omnibus 207, 213, 215
The Snow was Black 101
The Son 153
The Stain on the Snow 101
Stan the Killer 122
The Stowaway 94
Strange Case of Peter the Lett 9
Strange Inheritance 68
Strangers in the House 61
Striptease 161
Sunday 163
The Survivors 52

Talata 42
Teddy Bear 169
Three Beds in Manhattan 85
The Third Maigret Omnibus 144, 162, 196
Ticket of Leave 73
Tidal Waves 105, 128, 131
To Any Lengths 78
The Train 174
The Trial of Bebe Donge 72
The Triumph of Inspector Maigret 2, 17
Tropic Moon 24
Two Latitudes 18, 24

The Venice Train 193
Versus Inspector Maigret 160, 164
Violent Ends 128, 131

The Watchmaker of Everton 142
When I Was Old 214
The Widow 73
The Widower 171
A Wife at Sea 35
The Window Over the Way 27
The Witnesses 146
The Woman in the Gray House 28
The Woman in the Grey House 28

Young Cardinaud 69